PRAY ALONG PRAYERS

with

SUE HUGHES

Published by:
Keystone Productions
P.O. Box 8838, Huntsville, Texas
77340

All Scripture quotations are from the Holy Bible, King James Version. Certain pronouns in scripture that refer to the Father, Son and Holy Spirit may differ from other publisher's styles.

Co-Edited by Sue Gutierrez, Elizabeth Yielding
And Dr. and Mrs. Jim Sprague of Huntsville, Texas

Literary development and interior design by Sue Hughes
Cover design and cover artwork by Clay Harrell
"Calling all Christians to release the power of miracles through praying God's Word."
This book is published by:
Keystone Productions
P.O. Box 8838
Huntsville, Texas 77340
Printed in the U.S.A.
For information, call
1-936-295-6552

ABOUT THE AUTHOR

Sue Hughes

It is such an honor to offer my thoughts regarding my friend, Sue Hughes, and this anointed project that God has placed on her heart. Armed with an innate knowledge of the natural order of God for our bodies, Sue has always devoted herself to the familiarization of all that God has placed on the earth for our health and healing. Now, through this excellent prayer guide, she teaches us the provision of prayer that God has made for our spiritual sustenance.

Never has there been a better example of the adage, "Necessity is the Mother of Invention." This prayer guide began evolving during the illness and death of her husband, John. I have seen Sue's faith in the power of His Word sustain her through many adversities during his illness and throughout this project as she applied the principles that she shares here to her own life. After John's death, God impressed on her that her work in this area, along with pray-along audios, would be of benefit to others in their times of need. The obedience and total devotion to the completion of this project has been an inspiration to all that know her.

I possess an excitement and sense of the promise of miracles that will come forth into each person's life as they pray along with Sue and tap into the power of prayer that God has made available to each of us.

Sue Gutierrez

DEDICATION

To my Lord and Saviour, Jesus Christ, "My Goodness and my Fortress; My High Tower, and my Deliverer; my Provider, my Shield, and He in whom I trust;" Psalms 144:2

To my wonderful and magnificent mother, Lettie Croom McGee, and her equally wonderful and magnificent sister, my Aunt, Olice Croom Denmon, ages 93and 91, respectfully. These precious ladies, both like mothers to me, were an unbelievable fortress with which God blessed me. They showed by example, joy, peace, caring, integrity, and character. They were love in my childhood, and they are still love to me now. They showed the rewards of living for Christ, by their daily lives. They are *real Apostolic, Pentecostal Christians* with awesome faith, humble spirits, and the brightest of futures. I thank God, for blessing me with this wonderful Christian Heritage. And I thank you, Aunt Olice and Mom, for a world full of love and care.

Last, but not least, To God's children, for whom I have dedicated the last several years, preparing these prayers and scriptures. These prayers will help sustain you and make you stronger with each passing day, as you keep the Word in front of your eyes and in your ears. This book was written to assist you in calling forth your divine purpose and your day to day walk with the Lord, so that you might accomplish a more fulfilled life - a life filled with health, joy and prosperity and a life lived closer to God.

TABLE OF CONTENTS

IN MEMORY OF

John Bob Hughes

1944-2003

MEMORIAL

The late John B. Hughes, a master builder, Project Manager, and Superintendent of construction. John constructed buildings ranging in size from homes to major multi-storied high- rises. He was a man of vision, a man of great character and integrity, whose word was his bond. My husband of 15 years, my very best friend, through whom God blessed me and through whom He demonstrated His never wavering, unconditional love. A man whose memories are a wonderful part of my daily life and a part of my children's daily lives. A man who loved greatly and who is greatly loved. I can't help but wonder, for what magnificent assignment God needed him? I also wonder if his building materials have since changed to jasper, jade, marble, silver and gold. His being there makes Heaven a more priceless place to look forward to.

ACKNOWLEDGEMENTS

Three years ago, I thought I was compiling prayers and scriptures to stand on for my family, friends, my husband (who had the greatest need of all) and myself. I suppose God knew if He gave me the whole picture at one time, I might have gone in a different direction. For me, this was uncharted territory. It is amazing how God leads you, pulls you along (kind of like an inchworm, inching along), until you are far enough to get the picture of the project and be comfortable with that which He wants you to do. If I had known in the beginning how very time consuming this was to become, I may not have persisted. It has given me an awesome sense of responsibility, trying to make sure of the accuracy of every scripture and every word.

We are told by many, that when God gives you a project, a vision, a dream or an idea, that He will provide the people and the means of bringing it to fruition...that we just have to do our part and He will do the rest. I believe this to be true, because God has put ,and is putting, people into my path to help with this undertaking.

We know that we are the sum total of all the people we have met, known, and from whom we have learned. This book is no exception. There have been many ideas, works, perspectives, and thoughts given me throughout the years, which have given me part of the knowledge within this book; the rest of the material came from the Holy Bible through the direction of the Holy Ghost.

It seems that God has been setting me up all of my life, to be able to do this which He has called me to do; and, He has placed some "extraordinary people" in my life's path who have helped me, which I now give honor and thanks to: The Apostolic Pentecostal pastors, ministers and saints of my youth, (which was spent in central Louisiana). I experienced there, many services filled with the electrifying anointing of the Holy Spirit; and saw many healed, of all kinds of sicknesses and diseases. I am truly thankful for my "Ole Time Pentecostal" roots and upbringing, and for the love and care I received from the wonderful ministers and saints, whose greatest desires were to win souls and just to be used up for the Lord. I thank you all.

I wish to thank Shane McWhorter, who is like another son to me and a wonderful, delightful young man. He is my computer genius and has made this project much easier and quicker than it would have been without his knowledge and assistance. I also thank Dennis Baldwin for his computer expertise, assistance, and the encouragement of both Dennis, and his lovely wife, Margaret Levy Baldwin.

To Sue Gutierrez, Elizabeth Yielding and Dr. Jim and Mrs. Debbie

Sprague, my excellent co-editorial advisors, I thank and appreciate you immensely for your expertise and willingness to help with this project. Your efforts are a true gift of love to those who will read this book. Most of all, I thank you for the treasure of your friendship.

Danita and Jim Cunningham, two of my three wonderful children, I thank you for your understanding, patience, and for all of your assistance, while I spent day after day, year after year, mostly writing, studying and reading the Bible. You are both treasures beyond compare, irreplaceable, and I love you both immensely. I also thank you Jim, for being my sounding board and my mainstay.

Many thanks to a few of the special people in my life, who have encouraged me, prayed for me and lifted me up during this time; Pat Martinez, Frances Myers, Katie and Charles Lynch, Trenda Coburn, my cell group members, the church prayer group, my mother, Lettie McGee, and my Aunt, Olice Denmon. I also thank all of my other friends who have encouraged, and prayed for me.

I thank God for TBN, for DayStar, and the awe-inspiring line up of Ministers they present, from whom I've learned many wonderful things about God's Word.

I acknowledge my pastors, Jeff and Eileen Hackleman. Words seem scarce when I try to briefly convey how truly wonderful they both are. Pastor Jeff's teaching and preaching have left an indelible imprint upon my mind, heart and soul. His delivery is anointed, exceptional, supernatural, always fresh, and leaves me inspired, blessed and ready to face what ever comes. Jeff and our anointed, enthusiastic, beautiful and loving Eileen, make a superexcellent team! They are always uplifting, encouraging and supportive of their church family and all of our endeavors. I love and appreciate them, and I am so very thankful that they are my pastors and a part of my life. Thank you Jeff, for writing the "Foreword" to my book.

Last, but definitely not least, I give thanks and appreciation to my amazingly incredible, one- of- a -kind friend.....Sue Gutierrez, one whom God uses phenomenally. Thank you Sue, for all that you have done for me. Thank you for holding my John's hand his last two nights while letting me rest, and then for being one of the speakers at his funeral. You are so awesome, so very talented, with great wisdom, understanding, ability and loyalty. You are one whom the gifts of the Spirit definitely move in and work through. I thank you for being there for me in, oh, so many ways, and for your support, encouragement and excitement over my project. You can't imagine how much I appreciate, love, and thank you for everything. You add such great dimensions to my life.

FOREWORD

It is with great joy that I am writing the Foreword on Sue Hughes' book, which contains compelling insight about prayer. Prayer is the most awesome, powerful force in the universe. Prayer makes the dynamic power of God, available to us.

Eileen and I have known John and Sue Hughes for over thirteen years. Their love for God and faithfulness to His Kingdom has inspired my family, and I, to a great extent. One of my recipes for life is to love God, love family, love people, and love life. John Hughes will be remembered as a man who pursued this recipe.

Sue's book, *PRAY ALONG PRAYERS*, is a most unique training manual that does more than just teach on prayer; it leads you by the scriptures through the different kinds of prayer. You will learn how to pray by simply praying along with any of the well thought out, dynamic prayers in this book. It is my belief that this book should be in every home in the world!

All of the Daily Prayers are written by the pattern given in *The Lord's Prayer* by which, we are admonished to pray. You will be blessed by all of the Prayers, and will conveniently find many, many scriptures, on which to stand, for each subject.

As Christians, we must stay focused, and contend for the will of God, for notable miracles to occur in our lives. There are battles and challenges in life, but the Lord will bless you through them all when you contend (fight), for the outcome, and stand on the written Word of God. God still has the recipe for manna - He can still provide!

Prayer is a powerful weapon of contention. Sue has not only written these prayers by contending for the outcome; these "Pray Along Prayers" are also written, offensively.

Praying offensively, will diminish the time, one has to pray defensively. The favor of God will be on your life as you follow along into the presence of the Lord, with any of these Prayers.

Prayer has the potential to change the world. There are no limits in time, space, scope, or impact, in prayer.

I believe the greatest, and the most anointed sermons, songs, miracles, and restorations will occur in the twenty-first century. I also believe the most powerful prayer warriors, and prayer armies, will come forth in this generation.

Prayer should always be authentic (from the heart), accurate (scriptural), and abiding (consistent). Prayer should also be prayed with a spirit of faith. In the pages that you are about to read, you will learn how to take your prayer life to a new level in those three areas. Let's get started, and change the world, through the prevailing force of prayer!

Jeff Hackleman
Senior Pastor, Family Faith Church, Huntsville, Texas

INTRODUCTION

There is a great need over all the world for prayer.....

There is a great need in the body of Christ for prayer.....

There is a great need in the life of every believer for prayer.

These prayers are based on God's Word, which we know, is His will. I started writing these prayers at least three years ago as needs arose in my life. I asked God to show me how to construct the most effective way to pray concerning crises in my life; and to show me the most effective, powerful daily prayer that I could pray. I began to understand that we all live life at a very fast pace, and when confronted with a crisis, we don't always have the time, nor sometimes the means, to quickly find a scripture or scriptures to stand on with which to defeat our enemy.

Scripture after scripture have been compiled and used in these prayers; or have been given following the prayers, for you to stand on. Praying these prayers in earnest, while declaring God's Word over you, and your circumstances will bring abundant life, health, happiness, prosperity; all the blessings of God's covenant to you, when you live for God, keep His commandments, pay your tithes, and stand. God's Word never fails. When you pray God's Word in faith, believing and doubting not...you can have whatsoever you say! Praying my Daily Prayers, whether it be the one hour, the twenty minute, the ten minute or the five minute version, will cover you spiritually, physically, financially, emotionally and socially. I encourage you to pray along with me. Become intimate and comfortable with my book, *PRAY ALONG PRAYERS*, so you can keep up when praying the prayers on your CD. Pray along with your heart, mind, soul, spirit, and stay focused on our Lord Jesus Christ, fully expecting the miracles for which you pray!

These prayers are assembled for different needs; you can pray along with me, or you can play them in the background as you do other things. Pray along as you go back and forth to work or other places - as you wash dishes, work out, or go about your daily business. Find your own special time to pray along with me. Mix your faith with God's faith as you are speaking His Word. God's Word ministers life, and it ministers power unto us. It refreshes, nourishes, and heals our minds, hearts, and our spirits. God's Word is life changing!

Sue Hughes

PART I. Prophetic Revelations

Chapter One

A Prophet's Visit

On, Monday, March 29, 2005, the day after Easter, a most unusual, awesome, thing occurred which has prompted me to stop, write, and add this chapter to my book. For all practical purposes, my writing for this project was almost completely finished. By adding a few more scriptures here and there, I thought it would be ready for the printing and recording phase.

But God had other plans! It is totally amazing how God can get your attention when He wants to tell you something. It is also amazing how He knows how to find you! Pastor Jeff says that you do not have to go looking for Him; He will find you. How very true!

On that day, I was given a divinely imparted message, delivered by a most unusual appearing Prophet of God…one so un-ordinary looking that this occurrence reminds me of the scripture that admonishes us to be careful, lest we entertain angels unaware.

As I was seeing my friend, Frances Myers, to her car on this beautiful, sunshiny spring day, I noticed an unfamiliar Mercedes slowing down to turn into my driveway. I told Frances that I didn't recognize the approaching car and was relieved when she agreed to stay a few minutes longer since I was currently home alone.

My first impression was that this couple seemed friendly, peaceful, calm natured, and serene. When I saw the man, I remember thinking that he could possibly be a movie star or rock star. I could tell that he was definitely someone out of the ordinary with his dreadlocks and flamboyant personality.

He asked if my Mercedes, which had been put out close to the road, was for sale. I told him that it was, and offered the unusual story of the old car. His focus seemed to shift from the car, said that he would look at it on the way out, and then introduced himself and his friend to us. His name was Grady, hers was Angela; he said that she was "an angel" and that she went to Oral Roberts University. Grady told my friend and I that he had researched and developed the original anointing oil from the Bible, "The Holy

Anointing Oil" ® of Exodus 30:28. Grady said that he had recently started a company called the "Christian Oil Company" ®, to market the oil and had started marketing it to bookstores. "Praise God," said both Frances and I at the same time. They gave us a sample and a brochure on the oil, which made his story credible.

As the conversation progressed, I learned that Grady used to attend Family Faith Church, the local non-denominational church of which I am a member. He had moved a couple of times and had pastored a church in Madisonville briefly. He was currently ministering on the streets; Frances now knew, as I knew, that they were O.K., and she left.

As Frances was driving down the driveway, the most surprising and incredible thing happened. Grady said, "God wants me to tell you that He has you working on a project and that He wants you to finish it! He says that He wants you to finish it now, quickly, that He wants it out there!" For what seemed to be ten minutes at least, Grady just kept telling me how God wanted my project finished! I remember standing there in awe, thinking, "My God, you sent this man all the way out here to tell me to finish my project! You sent him to my home, and even had a friend posted outside with me when he drove up, so that I would talk to him!" He sounded like my son Jim, who all along has been telling me, "Hurry, Mom, finish your book. It needs to be on the market." Grady kept insisting that the Lord wanted my project finished now! What utter confirmation! What a miracle.... this man, whom I probably would not have ever even talked to under normal circumstances (and surely did not know), had been sent by God, way out in the country to tell me things that only God could be telling him. Wow! I was just blown away. I really thought that the first phase of my project was within a few days of being finished, but God had other ideas.

After several minutes of Grady stressing the importance of me finishing the project, I knew, without a doubt, that God had sent him. And he thought that he'd stopped to see my car. Grady, knowing that I was quite shocked by all of this, told me that with his ministry on the streets, this type of occurrence was nothing out of the ordinary for him and that he has had the gift of prophecy for a long time. *"Let me assure you, it certainly was out of the ordinary for me."* I knew, however, that God really did send him and I felt comfortable enough by this time to share with them the details of my project and invited the couple into my office. I told them that I was working on a book of prayers and asked if they would like to see it. When I handed Grady the book, he looked at it with a sense of familiarity…. as though he knew that this was the project about which he was telling me. As he held it between his hands with his head bobbing up and down, he was saying, "Yes, yes, yes… this is it… this is it! God wants it finished; He wants it out there now." As he was holding my book, he said, "This is not all. You are going to be traveling and speaking extensively also."

Grady then said the most surprising thing to me. He said that God wanted to heal my faith; that my faith had been shaken and wounded badly. He added that this had hurt me inwardly and emotionally, and that God wanted to deliver me from that hurt. I have never before heard of, or thought of one's *faith* being hurt, or healed. He started telling me that faith cometh by hearing, and hearing, and hearing by the Word of God. That what you hear is what builds your faith. With his fingers in his ears, he said that we have to keep the Word in our ears to build our faith. I told him that amazingly, he was saying what I had written in my book!

Again, Grady said, "God wants to heal your faith!". Suddenly, I understood what God was trying to tell me…it was all about my husband John. I started telling him about my loving, wonderful husband, who had died from Non-Hodgkins Lymphoma cancer; he loudly said, "That's it! That's it!" That was why God wanted to heal me on the inside, that I had been terribly hurt, and needed healing. I told Grady that I had been raised old time Pentecostal and that I had seen people healed of diseases, from cancer to heart disease and everything in between. I had been healed many times myself, and I know that God is our Healer. I had expected Him to heal John, but he had died. I worked so hard and prayed continually, I found all kinds of scriptures on healing, wrote prayers, prayed daily (many times a day usually), and declared his healing from morning to night. I anointed with oil every bag of chemotherapy that went into his body (and there were many). I was doing everything I knew to do and continually studying to learn more about healing so that I could help him, I fought to keep him with me. You see, my husband was one in a million. He was so very, very wonderful. God showed me His unconditional love through John. Grady continued. He said that he knew that I had gone through an awful lot , both during the time of John's illness and since, and God wanted to heal me. He then put his fingers into his ears.

"What do you hear?" He asked.

I just looked at him.

"What do you hear? " He repeated.

Finally, I answered, *" I hear the Word!"*

He said, "Very Good!"

With his fingers still in his ears, he asked over and over,

" Now, tell me, what did John hear?"

I kept looking at him with my heart breaking. He kept asking,

"What did John hear?

What did John hear?

Tell me, what did John hear???"

The words that started out as a scream in my heart barely left my mouth as a whisper,

"John heard… the doctors!"

Grady started beating on my desk with his fist, rather radically, and shouted loudly, "PUT IT IN THE BOOK!!! PUT IT IN THE BOOK!!! PUT IT IN THE BOOK!!! PUT IT IN THE BOOK!!! PUT IT IN THE BOOK!!!!!"

Inwardly, I had known all throughout John's illness that he was listening to the wrong report, the report of the doctors. Although he wanted to have faith enough to be healed, he really thought that my faith and prayers would be enough to heal him; along with those of our loved ones, our cell group, church and our precious pastors, who were believing for his healing also. He thought that this would be more than enough to bring him through. I really thought that too. I was determined that God was going to heal John. It may seem strange to some that, having gone through those past three years with multiple hospitalizations and endless bags of chemo, and seeing his body go down little by little, that I was able to keep that faith. I ignored all of that because I knew then, and I know now, that God could have healed John instantly or that he could recover progressively, day by day. It did bother me though, that John believed that he could ask God one time and then just thank Him everyday, instead of asking until he received.

Grady said, "John's faith took him as far as he could go and then he went on." He said, "John is fine, and he is thrilled over what you are doing. He is applauding you from heaven. There is nothing that he wants more than for you to finish your project." He must have told me 30 to 50 times very adamantly, to finish my project, to stay focused, and not let anything distract me from working on it.

There was a Holy excitement present. You could feel the power of the Lord. It was as though you could have cut through the atmosphere in the room with a knife. The energizing presence of the Lord was euphoric and exhilarating. We visited a while, talking about the Lord. They said that they only had a few minutes when they arrived, but they stayed two to two and a half hours, yet it seemed like only a few minutes.

Everyone who has been a guest in my home knows that I have this precious, white toy poodle named "Popeye," who barks and alerts me when anyone comes and continues to do so until they stop and pay attention to him. He even barks at family members upon arrival, until we stop and love on him a little. To my amazement, Popeye did not bark the first time at them. He was outside when the couple drove up, and inside with us when Grady was banging his fist on my desk and very loudly shouting for me to, "Finish the book, Finish the book."

Later in the den, Popeye lay on the hearth in front of Grady, sound asleep! I explained this to Grady who laughingly commented, "That's the Holy Ghost."

During the past few months, the enemy has been coming against me with pain in my lower back and in both legs. This had become increasingly worse in the weeks immediately before Grady and Angela's visit, so I decided to take advantage of the electrifying power of God which was manifested in our presence, and asked them to pray for my back. I thought if my back was healed, then my legs would be fine also, so I did not ask for healing for my legs.

Grady said that Angela was the one that should pray for me because she had the gift of healing! We stood in the middle of my den. She anointed me with "The Holy Anointing Oil"®, and prayed a powerful prayer! I remember thinking," Wow, she sounds like R.W. Schambach!". Angela bound and cast out the spirit of infirmity from me that, she said, had come to try to stop my project. It seemed to be getting close to stopping me at times!

I am glad to report that my back pain left immediately and has not returned, which to me is a miracle! Even though the pain in my legs has remained, I realized a couple of days after their visit that my legs were hurting less. Everyday, since beginning to write this chapter, the pain has diminished, *Praise God*, and I am recovering. I know that I will soon be completely whole!

Chapter Two

John Bob

John Bob Hughes and I married in 1988, and moved from Houston to Huntsville, his hometown, to escape the big city, build a home for us, and start a construction company. John's background was in Building and Construction Management. He started the first sub-division in the Champions 1960 area in Houston, and then graduated to larger and larger commercial projects. He built hospitals, schools, part of the nuclear power plant, and multi-storied buildings (his tallest high rise was 28 stories). John was always easy to spot on his projects, whether they were in Dallas, Houston, or other areas, because he was the one wearing a Gold hard hat.

John and I both gave our hearts to the Lord Jesus as young children. He was raised Baptist, and I, Pentecostal. I received the Baptism of the Holy Ghost at the early age of seven and spoke in tongues for at least two hours, in an experience that I have never forgotten to this day.

As young adults, we married others, became busy with life and business and drifted away from our first love, Jesus. After marrying each other in 1988, our interest in the Lord was revived. We watched religious programs on T.B.N. Our hearts were stirred and we re-dedicated them to the Lord. We even listened to preachers in our travels. I also learned a new scripture... ***"I shall not die, but live, and declare the works of the Lord," Psalms 118:17.*** This scripture, coupled with knowing how to plead the blood of Jesus, and declaring that we are healed by the stripes of Jesus kept me very busy, for days, weeks, months and even years to come.

A few weeks away from finishing our home, John had a major heart attack. After suffering unrelenting pain for three days, which he thought was indigestion, he finally let me take him to the doctor. The doctor told me in the hall that he had started an E.K.G. on John and that he was having a heart attack. He called for an ambulance to take him those few blocks to the hospital. The first thing out of my mouth was, "May I use your phone to make a long distance call to my mom?"

You see, I have been blessed all my life to have a praying mom who knows how to touch the throne of God. She also has faith in His healing virtue and the powerful blood of Jesus. She knows whom else to call, to get prayer going for a person or situation. Meanwhile, the ambulance came and was quickly getting John out of the doctor's office as I made my quick phone call to inform my mother what was happening and to ask for prayer. They were not able to get John stabilized at the local hospital all afternoon, so they life-flighted him to St. Luke's Heart Institute in Houston. He was in severe pain all this time, and was given morphine every few minutes from around 11:00 A.M. until 4:00 A.M. the following morning. I quickly drove to Houston, praying for John all the way. I <u>declared continually</u> while standing by his bed until 4:00 in the morning, that, "<u>John shall not die, but live and declare the works of the Lord. I plead the Blood of Jesus over John, from the top of his head to the soles of his feet, I apply the Blood of Jesus over John's heart and over his entire cardio-vascular system. I declare that John is healed, in Jesus name.</u>" It was 4:00 in the morning when he first experienced no pain. I later discovered that neither the doctors, nor his family had much hope for him.

I remember standing in the hall the next morning, talking with quite a few of John's family members. They were lamenting "what a shame it was, that we were losing John." They were talking like he was already in the dying process. I told them very adamantly that John was not going to die, that he was going to live! They were shocked! They looked at me so pitifully, like I wasn't accepting this fact that they all seemed to know. They looked rather concerned for me, as though I just didn't get it. I think they were wondering what they were going to do with me; because I wasn't accepting what they thought was a reality.

Then one of John's relatives spoke up and asked, "Sue, what makes you think that John is not going to die? The doctors do not give him any hope." I bravely told them all that "God was going to heal him; that he was not going to die!" This relative asked, "Do you really believe that God can heal John?", then said, "I was raised at such and such church in Huntsville, and heard preachers preach all of my life about people being healed, but I have never known of the first person that God ever healed." Thinking,"How sad!", I answered, "I know that He can, and that He is!" I went on to tell them that, growing up, I had seen people healed of heart attacks, knew people off whom cancers had fallen from their bodies, and all kinds of illnesses reversed. I had been healed many times, myself, of various things; and that God was going to heal John also. They all looked as though I had probably fallen off a turnip truck on the way to St. Luke's, but I didn't care. I knew that I had to be strong and believe for John, or he would die!

This is not meant to put down John's family in any way. They were all wonderful, outstanding persons, whom I loved. It is meant however, to show their lack of knowledge of the power and the healing virtue of Jesus Christ that is available to each of us, as His children.

John came home in a couple of weeks … his life was really changed! This tough, strong man, a former football star in his high school years, had been reduced to lying around on sofas all day; barely able to get up and walk around a little. I prayed for him, studied the Bible and nutrition; and tried to feed him the best I could, both spiritually and physically. He was just so very weak; and was all but totally bedridden. One year later, John had another heart attack.

After leaving St. Luke's again, we went back to Houston for a cardiologist visit. I will never forget this visit to the doctor's office. I think that it is permanently imprinted on my mind. With no outward show of sympathy, empathy, or caring at all, the doctor matter-of-factly informed John that he had lost the bottom 30% of his heart. He went on to say that he was probably one of the types of people who would continue to have heart attacks until there was nothing left of the heart! We were devastated and felt like someone had "pulled the rug," so to speak, out from under us. We were then dismissed to go home and handle this information the best way that we could. We were extremely stunned to say the least. We automatically went to our vehicle and started home.

I began getting angry... "Who", I asked John, "does he think that he is, playing God this way?" It does look like one of the premier diagnostic medical facilities in Houston could show their patients, and their families a little more concern and caring than this. We felt that we had been pushed out into the street to fend for ourselves. And, for us to go home, accept the fact that John was going to keep on having these terrible things called heart attacks, and then, just roll over and die was not acceptable to us.

As we started driving down the street, I declared that this was not going to happen, that he was not going to have any more heart attacks, and that he was going to get well! I declared over him then, and very frequently afterwards, "John shall not die, but live, and declare the works of the Lord. By the stripes and the blood of Jesus Christ, John is healed." John improved year after year. He recovered! He recovered amazingly well, *Praise God*! John recovered so very well that his heart was never again an issue, not even during or after taking all that chemotherapy, not even when he died. John was neither aware nor knowledgeable of the healing virtue of Jesus Christ until we married. He, like his family, definitely had never seen anyone healed, nor had he experienced healing himself. He was, I think, surprised, thrilled and so appreciative of his healing. John thanked the Lord daily for his healing; though he never, to my knowledge, boldly testified to others, with the exception of a few believers, about how Jesus had healed his heart.

One afternoon, after a daily nap during his recovery phase, John came into the kitchen/den where I was and stood speechless at the end of the cabinets. He looked as though "he had seen a ghost," as the old adage goes. He was very pale, but I didn't say a thing. I kept busy, looking at him frequently. After several minutes, he started talking, almost in a whisper. "Sue, you are not going to believe what just happened to me." He said that he was almost afraid to tell me about it, but he couldn't stand the idea of not telling me. John said that he was awakened with three (3) angels standing at the foot of our bed. They were beings of light. They were "completely, all over, bright, bright light. Their faces, their clothes, their whole bodies, were entirely bright, bright, bright light". They were angelic beings of pure white light. John just stared at them and never said a word to them; however, they had a message for him.

Their message to him was,

"*TELL THEM THE* TRUTH, *JOHN BOB, TELL THEM THE TRUTH!*"

They stood there for several minutes and then, just disappeared. John said they looked so real that it could not have been a vision, that he was awake, and that they were actually there. It amused me that he was so puzzled that they even knew his middle name, because no one used it in his adult life. Can you imagine God not knowing your middle name?

John wrestled with the message they brought for years, I suppose for the rest of his life. He said that he couldn't figure out who the "them" was, that they were referring to, and couldn't figure out what "the truth" was, that they wanted him to tell. It made a powerful impact on him though. I asked him if he thought that they wanted him to tell his family and others how God had healed his heart. He never acknowledged understanding their message.

Following the second heart attack and as soon as John was physically able, we started going to Family Faith Church in Huntsville, Texas, a wonderful church where we were always fed uplifting, faith building messages. John loved the Lord, and as I, always looked forward to Pastor Jeff's next sermon.

John continued improving until he was able to keep up with most of us. During the years of his recovery from heart attacks, I was busy taking care of John, studying the Word and compiling scriptures for different problems, sicknesses and such, and writing various prayers. I wished that we had had these types of prayers available when we were so overwhelmed with all these problems that attacked us, but we didn't. So, I felt compelled to prepare them for us. The thought of how prayers prepared for others could be of tremendous help to them in their times of need, came to me very frequently.

I believe that God extended John's life for the next thirteen years, almost as long as the fifteen years that He did for Hezekiah in II Kings 20:6.

The opportunity of talking with his very best friend, Chuck, was another thing that kept John going and kept him looking forward to the next day for many years. They laughed, planned, plotted, and reminisced every day. They had such great fun, they would laugh and talk for hours. Their daily visit was like most folks' cup of coffee.... necessary!

After living a fairly normal life for several years, John started having symptoms. The doctor diagnosed cancer- that most dreaded of diseases- specifically, Non-Hodgkins Lymphoma, cancer of the lymphatic system. I had always heard that if they could catch cancer before it reached the lymph system, there might be a chance of arresting it. But this was cancer of the lymph system itself, a really big one to deal with! We had just had another rug pulled completely out from under us.

John had watched his own dad die of cancer at the age of 55, so it was a frightening thing to him. He thought that his only hope would be in taking chemo and doing just what the doctors advised. He felt confident that this, coupled with all the prayer going on for him, would surely bring him through.

John battled this demon called cancer the last three years of his life. Very eagerly, he voraciously consumed one round of chemotherapy after another- over, and over, and over... until he was gone. All of the doctor's reports scared him. He bought into what they told him way too much. He just really believed that he had to take all of that chemotherapy.

I was determined that God was going to heal John of cancer, just like He had healed his heart. I studied the Word, wrote powerful prayers that I prayed daily over him, and searched out healing scriptures to declare over him. I wrote, collected and categorized groups of scriptures. I was not going to be defeated!

We were also faithful to attend our cell group meetings. These were led by Katie and Charles Lynch and held in their home. This was our other "family," who declared John's healing every Sunday night. Without the support of Katie, Charles, and our wonderful cell group members, I really don't know how we would have coped. This uplifted us, along with all the prayers from our faith-filled pastors, prayer warriors from the church, and other friends and loved ones. Friends, like Trenda Coburn, who prayed John's Special Healing Prayer every morning, were all so faithful to remember John and to pray for him. I don't know what we would have done without them. They also believed that God was going to heal John.

Those last several years were so hard. It was almost like a full time job going to Houston for round after round of chemo. I anointed every bag of chemo with oil, and prayed over them. I confessed that it would not make John sick, but that it would go in and kill every bad cell and not harm any of the good cells. It was amazing to us how he never experienced the nausea, infections, baldness or other horrible side effects that his fellow chemo patients were experiencing. However, he seemed weaker and weaker with each successive round of chemotherapy.

The last few years were consumed with staying busy and doing all that I could to take care of John. I prayed and believed that God was going to miraculously heal my amazingly wonderful John, but that didn't happen.

In the winter and spring of 2003, John's health seemed to be spiraling downward quickly. But I still knew that God was going to heal him. One morning in early July, I was awakened by a vision with a very tall, thin man, who was dressed in black. His suit, shoes, top hat, and gloves were completely black from head to toe. He was holding a small rectangular black box (which I knew contained instruments of harm), in his hands. He was taking long strides on our property, towards the house. I remember thinking, "I don't know if I can beat him back to the house or not, his legs are so long". I was quite a distance from the house and felt that I needed some sort of weapon with which to handle the matter. I did not think of him as the spirit of death, although I knew he was evil, and up to no good. I think I didn't recognize who he was because of the popular T.V. show that features the death angel all in white. I now know better...the spirit of death... wears black!

About a week later as I was preparing lunch, I went to the end of the kitchen to check on John, as was my custom. He was sitting in his favorite chair in the living room where he had been watching T.V. I was checking on him fairly frequently, because he wasn't feeling well at all. What I saw shocked and scared me! I sprang into action. John had no color in his face. All the blood had drained out of it. His eyes were closed, his jaw set. He was unmovable. I called him several times and received no response.

Another thing that I had been studying was how to raise the dead. In the event I was ever in a place where anyone needed to be raised from the dead, I wanted to be able to be used of God, to do it. I devoured anything I could find in the Bible or elsewhere on the subject.

Should anyone think that either I or my son, Jim, takes credit for raising my husband from the dead, I now give you Bible for what I believed happened. All we did was profess, claim, and speak God's Word in faith, with persistence, and God did the rest. God's Word still has the same power today, when we speak it, as it had when Jesus Himself spoke it. God's Word cannot fail. God cannot fail. We are told in **Isaiah 55:11,** *"So shall My Word be that goeth forth out of my mouth: it shall not return unto me void, but it shall accomplish that which I please, and it shall prosper in the thing whereto I sent it."*

John 14:12-14, *"Verily, verily, I say unto you,* **He that believeth on me, the works that I do shall he do also; and greater works than these shall he do; because I go unto My Father. And whatsoever ye shall ask in My name, I will do it. If ye shall ask anything in My name, I will do it."*

John 15:5, 7-8 *"I am the vine, ye are the branches;* **He that abideth in me, and I in him, the same bringeth forth much fruit: for without me ye can do nothing." "If ye abide in me, and My Words abide in you, ye shall ask what ye will, and it shall be done unto you." Herein is My Father glorified, that ye bear much fruit; so shall ye be My disciples."*

Matthew 18:18-20, *"Verily I say unto you, whatsoever ye shall bind on earth shall be bound in heaven: and whatsoever ye shall loose on earth shall be loosed in heaven. Again I say unto you,* **that if two of you shall agree on earth as touching anything that they shall ask, it shall be done for them of My Father, which is in heave***n. For where two or three are gathered together in my name, there am I in the midst of them."*

In **Matthew 21:21,22,** Jesus tells us to, *...have faith, and doubt not"*, and also, *If ye shall say unto this mountain* (our problems), *Be thou removed, and be thou cast into the sea; it shall be done. And all things, whatsoever ye shall ask in prayer, believing, ye shall receive.*

John 1:1 tells us that, *"...the Word was with God, and the Word was God."*
Hebrews 4:12,"For *the Word of God is quick (alive), and powerful."*

God's Word is anointed with His breath of life. His Words are a part of Him. Therefore, the written Word of God has the same ability, and the same authority when we speak it in faith, believing and doubting not, as it had when Jesus spoke it. In **John 10:35,** Jesus said that, *"...the scripture cannot be broken;"* and in **Numbers 23:19,** *"God is not a man, that He should lie; neither the son of man, that He should repent: hath He said, and shall He not do it? Or hath He spoken, and shall He not make it good?"*

We are also told in **Jeremiah 1:12,** *"Then said the Lord unto me, Thou hast well seen: for I will hasten My Word to perform it."*

I now put into practice what I had learned. Starting with binding Satan, all evil powers, the prince of the air, and the spirits of death and stroke; I commanded them to get away from John and off our property. I cast them all into outer darkness. I applied the blood of Jesus to John, and declared, John shall not die, but live, and declare the works of the Lord. I loosed the healing virtue of Jesus Christ into John's body from the top of his head to the bottom of his feet; throughout his cardio-vascular system, and throughout every cell and fiber of his being. I commanded the quickening power of Jesus to quicken his body over, and over, in Jesus name. Still praying, I ran to the kitchen door and called my son Jim who was working outside, to come quickly, and help me pray for John. He ran inside, and we both continued in warfare, in agreement with one another, praying for John's healing.

The blood gradually started coming back into John's face, and, after what seemed to be an eternity, he moved. *Praise God*! He was extremely weak though, and wanted to go to bed after a few minutes. He probably had to wait fifteen minutes or longer before he was strong enough to get up and walk to the bed. Meanwhile Jim and I were continually confessing his strength and healing.

The magnitude of what occurred that day I'm not over yet, and I'm not sure that I will ever be. I do believe that my husband was dead. At some point in this process, I called Katie and Charles, our dear friends, and cell group leaders. They came about forty-five minutes after John had gotten up and gone to bed. We all gathered around the bed, and prayed for him again. He slept all afternoon. He was drained, but he was alive!.

In July, John's only brother and sister-in-law were both killed instantaneously in a car wreck while he was in intensive care in Houston. For three days, his doctors had me keep this information from him because of the severity of his condition. I would leave his room to make phone calls to family members and then go back in his room with a smile on my face as though everything was all right. These were extremely hard times. John went through so very much.

After several more weeks, John was discharged. As exuberant as we were upon being home, we were devastated when we had to call an ambulance that same evening. In his own words, "we are losing control". Thank God through it all, John's mind remained sharp as a tack. He eventually wound up in intensive care again and, only three weeks after the deaths of his brother and sister in law, my John died.

The last two days of his life were extremely sad, like a bad dream, but at the same time... beautiful. He was surrounded with family and loved ones loving him; prayer warriors praying for him, and nearly all intermittently, singing softly to him, "Hal-le-lu-jah, Hal-le-lu-jah, Hal-le-lu-jah, Hal-le-lu-jah". This comforted and soothed him so. On and on, the beautiful songs that he loved so much continued with out musical instruments, with only with the sweet presence of the Lord accompanying them.

God's loving presence so filled the room that we knew angels were standing all around. We could feel them. The nurses and doctors felt that sweet presence too and remarked over how wonderful it was to see such a sight as this. They said they wished all of their patients could experience the love that they felt manifested towards John. Many of our good friends and loved ones had gathered around to pray for John and to comfort him. When they had time, some of the nurses and doctors would stand in the hall and listen to the beautiful, anointed singing. They said that they had never seen anything like this before, not on this scale... neither had I.

The day before he died, John was surrounded in the intensive care unit by our awesome pastors and many other friends drifting in and out of the room, with praying and singing continually on-going. John seemed so peaceful, as long as the singing continued. He knew that our Eileen's (Hackleman, Co-Pastor), and our dear Tracy Stoudt's beautiful voices were singing just for him. At some point during the day, John managed to get enough strength to say, "Don't let me die!" He just knew that our prayers would be enough to bring him through.

The doctors had told me that they believed he only had a few more days to live and that they had done all that they could do. Unless his kidney function improved over night, he was not going to make it. They sent Hospice to talk to me. I thanked them, told them I could not give up on him, and sent them away. I just knew that his kidney function would improve over night, and they would be able to stabilize him, and then he would get well.

The doctors said that there was no reason for him to stay in the intensive care room since there was nothing else they could offer him, except to try to keep him as comfortable as possible. They offered us an absolutely huge room, so that our family and friends could be together, instead of being spread out between the intensive care unit, and it's waiting room.

We all moved upstairs and were welcomed by more friendly nurses and staff. They brought in chair after chair, until all were seated. After we were on this floor for a few hours, his nurse told me that she wished she could just stay in John's room. She had never before seen anything or felt such a sweet presence like that in a patient's room before. She said that people more often were fighting, and so desperate at a time like this. Praise God for His helping power!

Thinking that John was going to be better by morning, I let my dear friend, Sue Gutierrez, talk me into spending the night in the nice room that she had gotten for me. I knew that she would take excellent care of him. She, along with two of our good friends, Bob Stoudt, and John Hawley, stayed with him that night.

All the next day, August 10, 2003, friends and family came and went, though they mostly came and stayed. By late afternoon, the room was filled with loved ones praying and singing like the day before. Around 7:00 P.M., Katie noticed that our entire cell group had come to see John, all at the same time, without being prompted by anyone, Each member had individually driven an average of twenty-five miles to the Conroe Hospital. John loved every member of his cell group. As sick as he was at times, he never missed a cell group meeting unless he was in the hospital.

These little cell group meetings were so very important to John. They were to me also. It was amazing and very appropriate, that his last night on earth was his last cell group meeting; although this time, his cell group had come to him.

This super-sized room was now filled with the dearest of friends and loved ones. Many were gathered around his bed for hours; Margaret Baldwin, leading often times with her pure soprano voice, was singing different songs that were so lovely, so warm and beautiful.

Again, it felt that you could just reach out and touch angels' wings as their presence undoubtedly filled the room. The sweet presence and love of the Lord was so uplifting. It felt like we were standing on Holy Ground, right there, in that hospital room.

The voices started once again singing ".Hal-le-lu-jah…..Hal-le-lu-jah…..Hal-le-lu-jah…..Hal-le-lu-jah…..Hal…le---lu---jah--.---!!" A Holy hush seemed to fill the room….such pure sweet love…….It was a very sweet home going for John. Without any effort, he just quit breathing…..and was immediately in the presence of the Lord.

Three days later, our wonderful Pastor, Jeff Hackleman, preached John's funeral. Two of John's best buddies, Mickey Evans and Roy Smith, who were schoolmates of John, from grammar school through college, also spoke, reminiscing about John and fun things that they as boys had done together.

Our friend, Sue Gutierrez, was also one of the speakers. She, of course, spoke eloquently. I asked her to read the poem that I had written about John the night before the funeral. In prayer, I asked the Holy Spirit to write something about John through me, that I could have Sue read. The following poem is what I was given. Isn't it amazing how the Holy Spirit just slipped in the part about how God healed John of serious heart disease? This poem was penned in about ten or fifteen minutes and was shared with several hundred people, his family, and friends. I include the poem now so you will have a better understanding of the depth of my wonderful husband and a little more knowledge about why I really do miss my loving, incredible John!

John Hughes
My Personal Angel

A man of strength.....
A man of valor..........
A man of courage beyond belief;

A man of integrity...........
A man of righteousness.....
A man so close and so dear to my heart;

A man of Great Faith.....
A man of Great Peace.....
A man God healed of serious heart disease;

A man who walked with God.....
A man who talked with God.......
A man of visions and creativeness, so rare;

A man who lifted others up.....
A man who loved all, and cared so very much...
A man you could trust, with all of your heart;

This man God gave to me for a guide, for a helper. A daily inspiration for all to see;
With a tear in my eye, and pain in my heart, I celebrate his departure, with a yearning to live like him; so that I may sit at the feet of Jesus, and sing praises with him.

"What Ifs About John's Angelic Visit"

WHAT IF John had told "them," (anyone, everyone), how God had miraculously healed his heart?

Revelations 12:11, *"And they overcame him (*the enemy*) by the blood of the Lamb, and by the word of their testimony,"*

WHAT IF John had told "them," about how God had extended his life like Hezekiah, thirteen years?

II Kings 20:6, *"And I will add unto thy days fifteen years;"*

WHAT IF John had told "them" "the truth," the truth about his healing?

Jeremiah 30:17, *"For I will restore health unto thee, and I will Heal thee of thy wounds, saith the Lord..."*

I Peter 2:24, *"Who His own self bare our sins in His own body on the tree, that we, being dead to sins, should live unto righteousness: by whose stripes ye were healed."*

Psalms 91:14-16, *"...Therefore will I deliver him: I will set him on high", "He shall call upon me and I will answer him: I will be with him in trouble; I will deliver him, and honor him. With long life will I satisfy him, and shew him my salvation."*

WHAT IF John had told "them" "the truth," the truth about God's Word? For God's Word is truth.

Psalms 119:170,172, *"Let my supplication come before thee: deliver me according to thy Word." " My tongue shall speak of thy Word: for all thy commandments are righteousness."*

God's Word is forever true, *"Ye shall know the truth and the truth shall set you free."* John 8:32.

Psalms 119:160 tells us, *"Thy Word is true from the beginning: and every one of thy righteous judgments endureth forever."*

WHAT IF John had chosen to receive God's most precious, priceless gift to mankind after salvation, whereby receiving power; The wonderful gift of the Holy Ghost!

Acts1:4,5,8, And Jesus, *"...being assembled together with them, commanded them that they should not depart from Jerusalem, but wait for the promise of the Father, which, saith He, ye have heard of me. For John truly baptized with water; but ye shall be baptized with the Holy Ghost not many days*

*Hence... **But ye shall receive power, after that the Holy Ghost is come upon you: and ye shall be witnesses unto me...***"

I can't help but wonder if he had, would he still be here today? I don't know, but I think that he would. I do know that John is safe, happy, and healed in heaven. For that, I am most, most grateful!

I had no intention of writing the two previous chapters. This was private information, I thought, only for my family and close friends. Although I had promptings in my Spirit at times to write about John - I dismissed them.

Not until God sent His prophet, Grady, to tell me very adamantly to,

PUT IT IN THE BOOK,

PUT IT IN THE BOOK,"

did I ever really consider putting it in the book!

The book I thought was practically finished, when Grady came to visit. My son, Jim Cunningham, and our friend Shane McWhorter, my computer guru, both after reading what are now the first two chapters said, "Yes, this has to go in the book." Jim said, "Mom, this is what the book is all about, this is the beginning of the book!" My Spirit felt a check; I knew after thinking about it for a few minutes, that he was right; it was the beginning of the book. Isn't there a scripture about the last being first, and the first being last? God certainly gave me the first two chapters of this book... last.

I pray that a chord will be struck in your heart by these prayers, and that these prayers are only a beginning for you. I hope that you will cover you and yours with the Daily Prayer of your choice, whether your schedule allows you one hour, twenty minutes, ten minutes or five minutes. I pray, too, that you continue in praise and worship to your creator in relational prayer. Pastor Jeff aptly claims that having a relationship with God is what prayer is all about. My prayer for you also is that you pray out the mysteries of God in the Holy Ghost, the Holy Spirit.

Trusting these individual prayers will be a blessing for you in your prayer life. May God bless and keep you, and cause His light to shine upon you.

Part II. Revelations of Our Authority

Chapter Three

The Word

When Jesus was on earth he prayed...and then he went forth performing miracles and preaching, speaking the Word - God's Word that He left for us. **Mark 1:35** *"And in the morning, rising up a great while before day, He went out, and departed into a solitary place, and there prayed."*

We must get the Word in our hearts to speak with our mouths like Jesus did, so that miracles can be performed in Jesus' name.

Joshua 1:8 tells us, *"This book of the law shall not depart out of thy mouth; but thou shalt meditate therein day and night, that thou mayest observe to do according to all that is written therein: for then thou shalt make thy way prosperous, and then thou shalt have good success."* To be able to co-create with God, we must be full of the Word. We must keep the Word of God on our tongue. Our cup must be full and running over. Our spirit has to be on fire for God. Our spirit man must be strong, and full of the peace, joy, and the praise of God. We have to practice speaking and receiving God's Word. We need to keep the Word in our hearts, for it is life, and it is health to all of our flesh; then, we are promised wealth and prosperity. In **Matthew 21:22,** we're told, *"And all things, whatsoever ye shall ask in prayer, believing, ye shall receive."*

Also, to be effective in our prayer life, we must put on our armor daily, to protect ourselves, and we must tear down the enemies' strongholds, and all of his powers. **Jeremiah 1:9, 10, 12,** *"Then the Lord put forth His hand, and touched my mouth. And the Lord said unto me, Behold, I have put my Words in thy mouth.*

See, I have this day set thee over the nations and over the kingdoms, to root out, and to pull down, and to destroy, and to throw down, to build, and to plant." "Then, said the Lord unto me, Thou hast well seen: for I will hasten my Word to perform it."

God placed His Words in Jeremiah's mouth to destroy the

enemy: God has given us His Word also, the written Word of God, which He tells us to put into our mouths. It is also our responsibility to use His Word to destroy our enemies. God has called us to be holy warriors, to block the enemy before he can attack and He has called us to take back that which the enemy has stolen.

Luke 21:15, *"For I will give you a mouth and wisdom, which all your adversaries shall not be able to gainsay ([dispute, disprove, overcome) nor resist"* (prevail against, oppose, question nor defy). God has given me a mouth and the wisdom to use His Word, the sword of the Spirit, the shield of faith, and the whole armor of God, to effectively block, and defeat Satan, and all evil on every hand. The most powerful weapon we have, and the most forceful weapon we have is our tongue. In James, chapter three, James explains how a bit in the mouth of a horse causes him to go in the right direction. Also, a rudder can guide a whole ship in the right direction. Our tongue can also be a powerful force for good or evil. The tongue can control our whole body, our emotions, and our thoughts. Our tongues can lead us into paths of success and prosperity. Proverbs states that the tongue has the power of life, and death.

When we speak, either the angels are sent forth to perform the Words we've spoken or our words are acted on by evil. Eve disobeyed God and spoke against that which God had commanded before Satan could start performing destruction to our world, and our lives. When we speak positive words and declare the Word, all heaven stands at attention and the angels carry out our decrees. God said that He watches over His Word, to perform it.

We have great power! Let us start using it effectively to tear down the enemy's strongholds and make his warfare against us non-effective.

Jesus commanded the apostles in **Matthew 10:7, 8,** to *"Go preach.... Heal the sick...raise the dead, cast out devils."* Shortly afterward, Jesus sent seventy others out to preach the gospel, and to heal the sick. In **Luke 10:17,** they declared upon returning, **"Lord, *even the devils are subject unto us through thy name."*** Throughout Matthew, Mark, Luke and John, Jesus demonstrated power over all sorts of demons. In **Matthew 10:1** Jesus *"...called unto Him His twelve disciples, (*and*), He gave them power* *against unclean spirits, to cast them out, and to heal all manner of sickness and all manner of diseases.*"

In **John 14:12,** Jesus left his followers with a wonderful promise: *"Verily, verily, I say unto you, He that believeth on me, the works that I do shall he do also; and greater works than these shall he do; because I go unto my Father."* This is a promise unto us of greater miracles - an increase in the miraculous! Jesus, then teaching them in **Matthew 28:20**, "*...to observe all things whatsoever I have commanded you: and, lo, I am with you alway, even unto the end of the world.*

The last commission of Christ to His followers was, "*...Go ye into all the world, and preach the gospel to every creature. He that believeth and is baptized shall be saved; but he that believeth not shall be damned. And these signs shall follow them that believe; In my name shall they cast out devils;*" "*...they shall lay hands on the sick and they shall recover,*" **Mark 16:15-18. In Mark 16: 20, (These disciples)** "*... went forth, and preached everywhere, the Lord working with them, and confirming the Word with signs following.*" Jesus gave his disciples "*...power and authority over all devils, and to cure diseases," Luke, 9:1.* He has given that same power, and authority to us today that He gave to His disciples.

In the first 30 years of Jesus' life on earth, He was in the preparation stage. He did not perform one miracle, He did not heal the sick, nor did He cast out devils. The miraculous started functioning in His life when He followed the move of God on the earth at that time; He went to John the Baptist for baptism.

Acts 10:38, "*...God anointed Jesus of Nazareth with the Holy Ghost and with power: who went about doing good, and healing all that were oppressed of the devil; for God was with him."* In **Acts 1:8,** Jesus told his disciples, *"But ye shall receive power after that the Holy Ghost is come upon you:"* The early church was full of the Holy Ghost, meaning they were baptized by the Holy Spirit. They had power, the power of God. They then went forth performing miracles, healing the sick, and casting out devils.

Jesus waited until the Holy Ghost descended on Him like a dove, before going forth, and performing miracles, and He was the

Son of God! He also charged his disciples to wait until the Spirit had come to give them power, when they received the Holy Ghost. Then, shouldn't we also wait? Wait until we receive the Holy Ghost, so we will have power… that power over all the power of the enemy that Christ gives us? Let's lift up our voices like the early church did, *"And now, Lord, behold their threatenings: and grant unto thy servants, that with all boldness they may speak thy Word, By stretching forth thine hand to heal; and that signs and wonders may be done by the name of thy holy child, Jesus."* **Acts 4:29, 30.**

Jesus said in **Luke 4:18,** "*The Spirit of the Lord is upon me, because He hath anointed me to preach the gospel to the poor; He hath sent me to heal the brokenhearted, to preach deliverance to the captives, and recovering of sight to the blind, to set at liberty them that are bruised.*"

Jesus has given all the power that he used here on earth to His followers, and even more power. *"Behold, I give unto you power,"* **Luke 10:19** "*Verily, Verily, I say unto you, he that believeth on me, the works that I do shall he do also; and greater works than these shall he do;"* **John 14:12.** Jesus paid the price for that power at the same time He purchased our salvation. He defeated Satan and all evil. In **Colossians 2:13-15,** *"And you, being dead in your sins and the uncircumcision of your flesh, hath he quickened together with him, having forgiven you all trespasses; Blotting out the handwriting of ordinances that was against us, which was contrary to us, and took it out of the way, nailing it to His cross; And having spoiled principalities and powers, He made a show of them openly, triumphing over them in it."* **We are told in I John 3:8,** *"…For this purpose the Son of God was manifested, that He might destroy the works of the devil."*

Jesus has already destroyed the Devil and his works; He has already done the work. All we have to do is do like Jesus did… speak the Word! **Isaiah 49:2,** *"And He hath made my mouth like a sharp sword; In the shadow of His hand hath He hid me, and made me a polished shaft; in His quiver hath He hid me,"* As long as we live a consecrated life, full of the Holy Ghost, we can live a victorious life, a life filled with the miracle working power of Jesus Christ. We can live a life of victory.

As Christians, we have a choice in the way that we fight the enemy. <u>We can fight (pray), offensively</u>, blocking the enemy's attacks against us, preventing them from reaching us or affecting us. <u>We can also fight (pray), defensively</u>, as the enemy attacks us, putting out fires as we need to. It is my desire to block Satan on every hand, stopping him in his tracks; praying offensively, not giving him a chance to set up strongholds in my life.

The Lord has given us the means to destroy the enemy's plans and strongholds, as he tells us in **Isaiah 41:15**. *"Behold, I will make thee a new sharp threshing instrument having teeth: thou shalt thresh the mountains, and beat them small, and shalt make the hills as chaff."* And in **Matthew 11:12,** we're told, *"And from the days of John the Baptist until now the Kingdom of heaven suffereth violence, and the violent take it by force."* In **Mark 11:22-24,** *"And Jesus answering saith unto them, Have faith in God. For verily I say unto you, that whosoever shall say unto this mountain, be thou removed, and be thou cast into the sea; and shall not doubt in his heart, but shall believe that those things which he saith shall come to pass; he shall have whatsoever he saith. Therefore I say unto you, What things soever ye desire, when ye pray, believe that ye receive them, and ye shall have them."*

The disciples couldn't pray with Jesus one hour. Jesus asked Peter in **Matthew 26:40,41,** "And He cometh unto the disciples, and findeth them asleep, and saith unto Peter, What, could ye not watch with me one hour? Watch and pray, that ye enter not into temptation: the spirit indeed is willing, but the flesh is weak." <u>In order for us to be real overcomers, we must pray...we must discipline ourselves to pray, and we must plant seed. God's Word is seed; we have to get God's Word, God's seed, into our hearts to be able to co-create with God. God is forever faithful to his Word, He watches over it to perform it.</u> Let us declare God's Word over our lives, our children, our circumstances and our futures.

In this day and age, almost everyone lives life at a very fast pace. It takes so much of our time to keep our families' routines on track, that we don't always have the time to search the Bible for the scriptures we need to stand on, for any, or for all of our needs.

We know also that there is awesome power in unity. In

Ecclesiastes 4:12 we are told, " **And *If one prevail against him, two shall withstand him; and a threefold cord is not quickly broken.*** " It is my experience that the most effective prayers are those that are backed up, that are based on the Word of God, and those that we pray in agreement with another. Jesus tells us in **Matthew 18:19, *"Again I say unto you, That if two of you shall agree on earth as touching any thing that they shall ask, it shall be done for them of my Father which is in heaven."***

I have assembled prayers for different needs, which you can pray along with me, or for you to play in the background as you are doing other things. The Word will get into your heart. <u>That seed, the Word, must get into our hearts if we are to be effective in our prayer life.</u> As we pray God's Word together, as we make our declarations, I am in agreement with you and the Word that we are praying. <u>The two of us, agreeing with the Word, makes our prayer most effective</u>.

Listen to the Word, memorize it, study it, and speak it.

II Timothy 2:15, *"**Study to show thyself approved unto God, a workman that needeth not to be ashamed, rightly dividing the Word of truth**."* Show yourself approved unto God, which is your reasonable service. We know for sure that our God is faithful to perform His promises. We are told in **Deuteronomy 7:9, *"Know therefore that the Lord thy God, He is God, the faithful God, which keepeth covenant and mercy with them that love Him and keep His commandments to a thousand generations."***

<u>As you pray along with me (with your C.D.'s, or with the book), mix your faith with my faith. Most importantly, mix your faith with God's faith, as you speak God's Word. Let's commit our lives to God and His Word</u>. His Word ministers power, and life unto us. His Word nourishes and heals our minds, hearts, our spirits, and it is life changing. Accept the challenge to pray God's Word offensively. Pray with me as frequently as you can, and experience all the good, that God has available for you.

Speaking the Word

Mark. 4:14 *"The sower soweth the Word."* **Proverbs 1:23** *"Turn you at my reproof: behold, I will pour out my spirit unto you, I will make known my Words unto you."* We know that God's will is His Word, **I John 5:14-15** *"...if we ask anything according to His will, He heareth us: And if we know that He hears us, whatsoever we ask, we know that we have the petitions that we desired of Him."* Whatever the Bible says is God's will, we can have, and, we should have faith to receive. We also know that Faith cometh by hearing God's Word. **Proverbs 4:20-22,** *"My Son, attend to my Words; incline thine ear unto my sayings. Let them not depart from thine eyes; keep them in the midst of thine heart. For they are life unto those that find them, and health to all their flesh."* And in Joshua 1:8, *"This book of the law shall not depart out of thy mouth; but thou shalt meditate therein day and night, that thou mayest observe to do according to all that is written therein: for then thou shalt make thy way prosperous, and then thou shalt have good success."*

Deuteronomy 30:10-15, *"If thou shalt hearken unto the voice of the Lord thy God, to keep His commandments and His statutes which are written in this book of the law, and if thou turn unto the Lord thy God with all thine heart, and with all thy soul. For this commandment, which I command thee, this day, it is not hidden from thee, neither is it far off. It is not in heaven, that thou shouldest say, Who shall go up for us to heaven, and bring it unto us, that we may hear it, and do it? Neither is it beyond the sea, that thou shouldest say, Who shall go over the sea for us, and bring it unto us, that we may hear it, and do it? But the Word is very nigh unto thee, in thy mouth, and in thy heart, that thou mayest do it. See, I have set before thee this day life and good, and death and evil."*

Let us be sure that we choose life and good. Let us put God's Word in our mouths, and in our hearts. Let us act on our faith, let us speak the Word! Let us not confess (not talk about) that which we do not have; let us confess, what we desire to have. In **John 16:23, 24,** Jesus said, *"…. Whatsoever ye shall ask the father in my name, He will give it you"* *"… ask, and ye shall receive, that your joy may be full*." We know to pray effectively we must pray the Word, because God watches over His Word to perform it. If we are not praying the Word, God does not hear us, and He does not respond to us. God said in **I John 5:14,15,** "…*if we ask anything according to His will*, (which we know is His Word)*, He heareth us. And if we know He hear, whatsoever we ask, we know that we have the petition that we desired of Him*." He also does not respond to our prayers, unless we pray in the name of Jesus. God said to do everything in the name of Jesus.

Jesus praying to our Father in **John 17:8** about mankind (you and me), said, *"For I have given unto them the Words which thou gavest me;"* and in **John 17:13, 14** and **17,** Jesus still praying said, *"And now I come to thee; and these things I speak in the world, that they might have my joy fulfilled in themselves. I have given them thy WORD;"* *"Sanctify them through thy truth: thy WORD is truth*." Praise God, Jesus spoke the Father's Words in this world and, He gave us the Father's WORDS that we might speak them also, and have our joy fulfilled in ourselves. God hasn't changed his mind, nor has He changed his method. When Jesus was on earth, He defeated all of the works of Satan with the Word, *"It is written*;" To receive of the Father, we have to do the same. It is our responsibility to study the Word, to see what Jesus did, and what He said. When we stand on God's Word and speak it with our mouths, it makes God's great awesome power work for us. We need to speak God's Word, believe God's Word which we're speaking, and declare the end result, that which we desire. When you discover God's will for your life, which is God's Word, speak it over your life, agree with it, praying in faith believing, God's anointing will change, and rearrange, what needs to be changed in your life.

Hebrews 11:3, *"Through faith we understand that the worlds were framed by the Word of God, so that things which are seen were not made of things which do appear*."

Isaiah 59:21, "As for me, this is my covenant with them, saith the Lord; My spirit that is upon thee, and My Words which I have put in thy mouth, shall not depart out of thy mouth, nor out of the mouth of thy seed, nor out of the mouth of thy seed's seed, saith the Lord, from henceforth and for ever."

Matthew 24:35, "*Heaven and earth shall pass away, but My Words shall not pass away.*"

Deuteronomy 8:3 "*...man doth not live by bread only, but by every Word that proceedeth out of the mouth of the Lord doth man live.*"

Hebrews 4:12, "*For the Word of God is quick* (alive) *and powerful, and sharper than any two-edged sword, piercing even to the dividing assunder of soul and spirit, and of the joints and marrow, and is a discerner of the thoughts and intents of the heart.*"

Psalms 119:130, "*The entrance of thy Words giveth light; it giveth understanding unto the simple.*"

Psalms 119:105, "*Thy word is a lamp unto my feet, and a light unto my path.*"

<u>NOTES</u>

Chapter Four

Taking Dominion

God created man on the sixth day of creation. We find in **Genesis 1:26, 27,** *"And God said, Let us make man in our image, after our likeness: and let them have dominion over the fish of the sea, and over the fowl of the air, and over the cattle, and over all the earth, and over every creeping thing that creepeth upon the earth. So God created man in his own image, in the image of God created He him; male and female created He them. And God blessed them, and God said unto them, Be fruitful, and multiply, and replenish the earth, and subdue it: and have dominion over the fish of the sea, and over the fowl of the air, and over every living thing that moveth upon the earth.* And in **Genesis 2:7, 8,** *"And the Lord God formed man of the dust of the ground, and breathed into his nostrils the breath of life; and man became a living soul. And the Lord God planted a garden eastward in Eden; and there He put the man whom He had formed."*

We, mankind, are the rightful heirs on earth because God made man, and breathed into him the breath of life, and put him on earth to rule and reign over all His handiwork. God has always breathed life into every man that He has made, even today. Man is made of spirit, and the dust of the earth. God gave man dominion over all the earth, and all things in it, all animals...everything. God placed a living spirit in every being that He made and put on earth.

God gave every man He made, a spirit with which to commune with Him (God). When Eve ate the fruit, mankind lost the dominion that God had freely given him. Satan stole man's dominion. That is why God sent His Holy Spirit to impregnate Mary, to bring forth Jesus,(the man and the Christ) to give the Holy Spirit the authority to be here without breaking the laws which God had established.

God sent Christ (His Holy Spirit) to be born on earth through Mary (dust of the earth) and God declared by an angel, that she would call him Jesus. Jesus, God's son, and man, defeated Satan, and all evil on the cross. In **Colossians 2:13-15** we are told; "***And you, being dead in your sins and the uncircumcision of your flesh, hath He quickened together with Him, having forgiven you all trespasses: Blotting out the handwriting of ordinances that was against us, which was contrary to us, and took it out of the way, nailing it to His cross; And having spoiled principalities and powers, He made a show of them openly, triumphing over them in it!***" And in **Galations 3:13-15,** Paul tells us, **"*Christ hath redeemed us from the curse of the law, being made a curse for us: for it is written, Cursed is everyone that hangeth on a tree: That the blessing of Abraham might come on the Gentiles through Jesus Christ; that we might receive the promise of the Spirit through faith.*"**

Jesus Christ, the son of God, defeated Satan while on earth by speaking His Father's Word, and He tells us to do the same. It is our responsibility as Christians to do as Jesus did while we are on this earth. We are to follow in His footsteps. We are to speak the Word and declare the end from the beginning as He did. We are told in **Isaiah 48:3**, "***I have declared the former things from the beginning; and they went forth out of my mouth, and I shewed them; I did them suddenly, and they came to pass.***"

In **Numbers 23:19, 20,** we find that, "***God is not a man, that He should lie; neither the son of man, that He should repent: hath He said, and shall He not do it? Or hath He spoken, and shall He not make it good? Behold, I have received commandment to bless: and He hath blessed; and I cannot reverse it.***" Let us take our rightful dominion over the earth and all things in it, as we are commanded.

Matthew 11:12, "And from the days of John the Baptist until now the kingdom of heaven suffereth violence, and the violent take it by force."

Chapter Five

Preparing For Battle

God created man in His image. Therefore, Satan hates us and wants to defeat and destroy us. We are warned in God's Word, that we have an enemy! In **I Peter 5:8,** *"Be sober, be vigilant; because your adversary the devil, as a roaring lion, walketh about seeking whom he may devour."*

Paul tells us in **II Corinthians 10:3-5**, *"For though we walk in the flesh, we do not war after the flesh:(For the weapons of our warfare are not carnal, but mighty through God to the pulling down of strong holds;) Casting down imaginations, and every high thing that exalteth itself against the knowledge of God, and bringing into captivity every thought to the obedience of Christ;"* And in **Matthew 12:29**, Jesus asks us, *"...how can one enter into a strong man's house, and spoil his goods, except he first bind the strong man? And then he will spoil* (plunder) *his house."*

Our battle isn't only against Satan., It is also with all the fallen angels which are Satan's demons. **Ephesians 6:12** *"For we wrestle not against flesh and blood, but against principalities, against powers, against the rulers of the darkness of this world, against spiritual wickedness in high places."*

Spiritual warfare is an essential strategy in which we must actively participate in order to be able to walk in victory in our daily lives. We are not left alone to fight our enemies: we have been given our own personal armor, and the all powerful, Supernatural Word of God, to defeat Satan and all of our foes. **Ephesians 6:10-18** tells us, *"Finally my brethren, be strong in the Lord, and in the power of His might. Put on the whole armor of God, that ye may be able to stand against the wiles of the devil. For we wrestle not against flesh and blood, but against principalities, against powers, against the rulers of the darkness of this world, against spiritual wickedness in high places."*

"Wherefore take unto you THE WHOLE ARMOUR OF GOD that ye may be able to withstand in the evil day, and having done all, to stand. Stand therefore, having your loins girt about with truth, and having on the breastplate of righteousness; And your feet shod with the preparation of the gospel of peace; Above all, taking the shield of faith, wherewith ye shall be able to quench all the fiery darts of the wicked. And take the helmet of salvation, and the sword of the Spirit, which is the Word of God: Praying always with all prayer and supplication in the Spirit, and watching thereunto with all perseverance and supplication for all saints;"
II Timothy 3:16, 17, *"All scripture is given by inspiration of God, and is profitable for doctrine, for reproof, for correction, for instruction in righteousness: That the man of God may be perfect, thoroughly furnished unto all good works."* We learn to be effective spiritual warriors by taking heed unto the Word of God and by praying the scriptures, like Jesus did. Jesus defeated Satan on the cross. <u>For victory over our enemies, we must learn to pray in the authority God has given us in His Word. We must speak the Word out of our mouths with authority on a daily basis, put on our armor, and be strong in the Lord, as we are admonished and pray</u>! Jesus prayed daily to receive instruction from His heavenly father; so should we. God has given us the authority and the power to win, to be victorious over Satan and his demons. <u>We must put on our armor daily and pray offensively, to be protected from the enemy and to win over him, to defeat him.</u>
In I John 3:8 we are told, *"...For this purpose the Son of God was manifested, that He might destroy the works of the devil."* God has made His power available to us: He made us heirs of God and joint heirs with Christ (meaning we share the same things with Christ). Jesus defeated all of His foes; <u>we also have been given power over all the power of the enemy! God has made the same winning power that Christ exhibited, available to us</u>.
Luke 10:19 *"Behold, I give unto you power to tread upon serpents and scorpions, and over all the power of the enemy: and nothing shall by any means hurt you."* And in John 14:12 Jesus said, *"...He that believeth on me, the works that I do shall he do also; and greater works than these shall he do; because I go unto my Father. And whatsoever ye shall ask in my name,*

that will I do, that the Father may be glorified in the Son."

It is time for the body of Christ to arise... to arise with great power, the power that God almighty has available to us. With God's power flowing through us, we can defeat Satan, cast out devils, heal the sick, and perform miracles in Jesus' name. Let us consecrate our lives to God so that His mighty working power and His authority will be available to us as believers.

Let us stand on God's Word and let us use our God given authority, in Jesus' name, to bind all evil forces against us. Let us bind Satan and his entire hierarchy completely away from us and cast into the sea all evil assignments against us, making all of Satan's warfare against us, of no effect.

Before going into battle, we put on the whole armor of God, then we bind Satan and all evil. We bind his whole kingdom, his entire hierarchy, every demon, in the mighty name and in the Blood of Jesus.

Joel 2:11, *"And the Lord shall utter His voice before His army: for His camp is very great: for He is strong that executeth His Word:"*

Joel 3:9, "Proclaim ye this among the Gentiles; Prepare war, wake up the mighty men, let all the men of war draw near; let them come up;"

Joel 3:10, *"Beat your plowshares into swords, and your pruning hooks into spears: let the weak say, I am strong."*

Luke 22:46, "...And, (Jesus) said unto them, why sleep ye? Rise, and pray, lest ye enter into temptation."

Jeremiah 46:3, *"Order ye the buckler and shield, and draw near to battle."*

Zechariah 4:6, *"...Not by might, nor by power, but by my Spirit, saith the Lord of hosts."*

Matthew 11:12, "And from the days of John the Baptist until now the kingdom of heaven suffereth violence, and the violent take it by force." We've been given the power and the authority to tear down the enemies' strongholds. In **Matthew 18:18** Jesus tells us, *"**Verily I say unto you, whatsoever ye shall bind on earth shall be bound in heaven: and whatsoever ye shall loose on earth shall be loosed in Heaven.***"* I stand on the Word of God that gives us the right and the authority to bind and to loose.

I also stand on **Mark 11:23,** which gives us the power to cast our mountains – our problems, all of our assignments from evil, into the sea. In **Matthew 12:29** Jesus asks us, *"...how can one enter into a strong man's house, and spoil his goods, except he first bind the strong man? And then he will spoil his house."*

Before we go into prayer, let us use our God- given authority, in Jesus' Name. Let us put on the whole armor of God and bind Satan and his entire hierarchy, completely away from us, and cast all evil assignments into the sea, making all of Satan's warfare against us of no effect!

We turn our thoughts to prayer, praise and worship, and to sowing the Word of God. We come to authenticate, to make real the authority of God over our lives by confessing His Word over us. It is not by our great ability, neither is it by our goodness that we are able to co-create with God. It is God's ability to work on our behalf when we speak His Word and make our declarations in faith. In **Ephesians 5:1,** we are told to follow (imitate) God, to follow Him as dear children. He spoke the worlds into existence with His Word and we are to speak our world, our lives, our futures into existence by also speaking His Word.

We are told to believe in God. Jesus said to His disciples in **Matthew 17:20,** *"...If ye have faith as a grain of mustard seed, ye shall say unto this mountain, Remove hence to yonder place; and it shall remove; and nothing shall be impossible unto you."*

I invite you to spend this time praying the Word along with me as you drive back and forth to work or other places. Pray the Word along with me while doing other things, washing dishes, cleaning the house, working out, mowing the lawn, or ideally, when you can fully concentrate. Anytime you can pray, God is listening. He said that His Word will not return unto Him void. The Word will accomplish that which it is designed to do when we speak it forth in faith believing, doubting not, and having confidence in God.

<u>NOTES</u>

Part III. MY DAILY PRAYERS

Chapter Six

Sweet Hour of Prayer

Introduction

These prayers are based on the scriptures, according to the outline given in the Lord's Prayer. Before we begin our daily prayer, let us prepare our hearts to come before our God, in Jesus' name.

You must connect with God; stir up the Holy Ghost within you, in order to have a dynamic prayer. You must have a heart connection with God Almighty and you must pray the Word in earnest in order to pray effectively. So, empty your mind of the cares of the world. Let go of all your worries and concentrate on and meditate on the Word, as we pray our daily prayer.

The Word is mighty and it is powerful and the Word is God! When you meditate on the Word and pray it from your heart, it is not just a form. It assures you of having the attention of and the ear of God. God watches over his Word to perform it.

Earnestly pray along with me, and expect your harvest. His promises to us are all "Yes", and "Amen", in Christ Jesus. Follow along with me as the angels of the Lord establish our words which are based on God's Word.

Putting on our Armor

I put on the whole armor of God of **Ephesians 6:11-18,** that I may be able to stand against the wiles of the devil. I put on the breastplate of righteousness, the helmet of salvation; my loins are gird about with truth, my feet shod with the preparation of the gospel of peace. I take the shield of faith to quench the fiery darts of the wicked and the sword of the Spirit, the Word of God, to defeat Satan on every hand. And in **Ephesians 6:19, 20,** *"And for me, that utterance may be given unto me, that I may open my mouth boldly, to make known the mystery of the gospel, for which I am an ambassador in bonds: that therein I may speak boldly, as I ought to speak."* And having done all, I will stand, as we are *instructed, in* **Ephesians 6: 14.**

I plead the blood of Jesus over me, from the top of my head to the soles of my feet, and throughout every system, and cell of my being.

I ask you, Lord, to place this same armor and blood protection on and around my spouse, my children, pastors, and our family members; and everything I bind and loose, I do also for each of them, in Jesus' name, Amen.

We come now Lord, to apply Your Word to our lives, and to frame our worlds, like Jesus did. I thank you that you have established angels to bring forth our decrees. *"Bless the Lord, ye His angels; that excel in strength, that do His commandments, hearkening unto the voice of His Word. Bless ye the Lord, all ye His hosts; ye ministers of His, that do His pleasure,"* **Psalms 103:20, 21.** I thank you, God, that, as we bind and loose and as we declare your Word, the angels of God are establishing our words because they are based on God's Word.

Binding Satan and All Evil

Reversing Curses

Thus saith the Lord God, in **Matthew 18:18,** *"Verily I say unto you, Whatsoever ye shall bind on earth shall be bound in heaven: and whatsoever ye shall loose on earth shall be loosed in heaven."*

I address, rebuke, and bind you Satan, every fallen angel and every demon from the pit of hell, including all principalities, powers, borders, rulers of the darkness of this world, spiritual wickedness in high places, all evil kings, peoples, nobles, nations, the prince of the air, and every evil power and spirit that you rule, command and have jurisdiction over; And I cast everyone of you into outer darkness, in Jesus' name.

I bind and cast into the sea every evil assignment from every evil spirit, their causes and effects on all levels, spiritually, physically, emotionally, financially and socially, in Jesus' name. I bind them from each of our souls, spirits, bodies, possessions, finances, businesses, occupations, communications, transportation, prayers, God's angels, our witness to others, and our stewardship. In Jesus' name, I cast them all into the sea according to **Mark 11:23.** Thus saith the Lord, *"For verily I say unto you, that whosoever shall say unto this mountain, be thou removed, and be thou cast into the sea; and shall not doubt in his heart, but shall believe that those things which he saith shall come to pass; he shall have whatsoever he saith"*

I declare and decree that neither Satan, nor any evil spirit has any place in us, or any power over us. In the name of Jesus Christ, I break and reverse all curses against each of us according to: **Galations 3:13, 14** *"Christ hath redeemed us from the curse of the law, being made a curse for us: for it is written, Cursed is everyone that hangeth on a tree: That the blessing of Abraham might come on the Gentiles through Jesus Christ; that we might receive the promise of the Spirit through faith."*

And **Colossians 2:13-15,** *"And you, being dead in your sins and the uncircumcision of your flesh, hath He quickened together with him, having forgiven you all trespasses; Blotting out the handwriting of ordinances that was against us, which was contrary to us, and took it out of the way, nailing it to his cross; And having spoiled principalities and powers, He made a shew of them openly, triumphing over them in it."*

I confess that our bodies are temples of the Holy Ghost, redeemed, sanctified, cleansed, blood bought, and justified by the blood of Jesus Christ.

I totally dismiss you Satan, all of your dominion, and every evil assignment against my spouse, children, pastors, our family members, and myself, in Jesus' name. I loose the anointing of God and the power of **Isaiah 10:27,** to destroy the yolk of evil and I declare that Satan is under our feet, in Jesus' name! I thank you, Lord, for setting us free. Amen.

Colossians 2:10 *"And ye are complete in him, which is the head of all principality and power:"*

Romans 8:2 *"For the Law of the Spirit of life in Christ Jesus hath made me free from the law of sin and death."*

SWEET HOUR OF PRAYER

Thanksgiving and Praise

Our Dear Heavenly Father, I come into your gates with Thanksgiving and into your courts with praise. I come by the Blood of Jesus that gives me the right and authority to come before your throne. I thank you, Lord, for your love, your mercy, grace, peace, and blessings. I thank you for the Holy Ghost, and for your anointing; I thank you, God, for everything. I ask Jesus, my Chief High Priest, to plead my declarations together with me before you, Father, that I may be justified, according to **Isaiah 43:26**, *"Put me in remembrance: let us plead together: declare thou, that thou mayest be justified."* I thank you, Lord, that you hear and answer my prayers. **Psalms 4:3,** *"But know that the Lord hath set apart him that is Godly for himself: the Lord will hear when I call unto him."*

I seek first the Kingdom of God and your Righteousness. Everything I pray for myself, I pray for my spouse, children, pastors, and family members. I ask you to name others, which you desire to pray for now, in Jesus' name.

I thank you, Father, that I know that you are the King of Kings, the Lord of Lords, the Lord of hosts. You are my Redeemer, my Shepherd, the Light of the world, the Alpha and the Omega, the Beginning and the End, and beside you, there is no other. You are the Lion of the Tribe of Judah, the Root of David, the Main Cornerstone, the Maker and Ruler of all, and Hallowed is thy name. I thank you, that you are my faithful God, my Healer, my Provider. You are Holy and just, my Deliverer, and I rejoice in you, oh God, and offer up to you a sacrifice of praise. I sing unto you and exalt your Mighty Name, *"...O Lord, my God, thou art very great; thou art clothed with honour and majesty."* **Psalms 104:1**

I thank you, Lord, that you are the author and finisher of my faith, the Prince of Peace, my Chief Mediator, and the Fulfiller of all our covenant promises. Your kingdom is an everlasting kingdom and your dominion is from generation to generation, **Daniel 4:3**. *"...Worthy is the Lamb that was slain to receive power, and* *riches, and wisdom and strength, and honour, and glory, and blessing."* **Revelation 5:12.**

My heart rejoices in you, oh Lord, and I delight myself in you. Thou art my Father, my God, and the Rock of my salvation, the First and the Last; and beside you, there is no God. I glorify and magnify thy sweet, and Holy name. I adore you, Lord, and shout "Hosanna!, Hosanna!, Hosanna!", to the King of Kings, and the Lord of Lords; my Saviour and my Redeemer!

John 1:1, *"In the beginning was the Word, and the Word was with God, and the Word was God!"* I thank you, Father, for your Word which I can read and when I speak it with my mouth, devils have to flee. I thank you, that I can speak your Faith filled Words, speak *"GOD"* out of my mouth, mix it with my faith, and mountains have to move when I command them, according to **Mark 11:23,** *"For verily I say unto you, That whosoever shall say unto this mountain, Be thou removed, and be thou cast into the sea; and shall not doubt in his heart, but shall believe that those things which he saith shall come to pass; he shall have whatsoever he saith."* And in **Isaiah 55:11,** *"So shall My Word be that goeth forth out of my mouth: it shall not return unto me void, but it shall accomplish that which I please, and it shall prosper in the thing whereto I sent it."*

I thank you, God, that we can co-create with you, when we speak your Words in Faith! I rejoice because my name is written in heaven, according to **Luke 10:20;** and I declare that I will rejoice, and be glad in this day that you have made. **Psalms 118:24.**

REPENTANCE

James 4:8 tells us to draw nigh to God, and He will draw nigh unto us. I dedicate and consecrate my life unto you; I seek your face and your desires for my life. **I Chronicles 28:9** says that if I seek thee, you will be found of me and that I am to serve you with a perfect heart and with a willing mind; this I do whole heartedly, Lord.

Dear Father, I ask you to reveal to me, if there be any bitterness, unforgiveness or sin in my life that could be an open door to the enemy. The Word says in **Luke 6:37,** *"Judge not, and ye shall not be judged: condemn not, and ye shall not be condemned: forgive, and ye shall be forgiven:"*

I repent before you, Lord, and ask your forgiveness of anything that I've done, said or thought unpleasing in your sight; I forgive others of their debts and offenses unto me, that I may be forgiven. Help me to trust always in you, with all of my heart, mind, soul and strength, and to acknowledge you always, so that you will direct my paths; to fear you and to forever depart from evil, according to **Proverbs 3:5-7.**

LOOSENING GOD'S BLESSINGS
And COVENANT PROMISES

Matthew 6:33, "*But seek ye first the Kingdom of God, and His righteousness; and all these things shall be added unto you."*
I seek first the Kingdom of God, and Your righteousness Lord; and all these things shall be added unto me. I declare and loose the Anointing of God for the power of the gifts of the Spirit to be operational in my life. I loose the manifestation of the Spirit of God and His Anointing, to impart unto me, according to
I Corinthians 12:7-11: The Word of wisdom, the Word of knowledge, faith, the gifts of healing, the working of Miracles, prophecy, discernment of spirits, tongues and interpretations, dividing unto me severally as you will, that I may profit with all.
I Loose God's Anointing for the power of **Ephesians 1:3** over me, "*Blessed be the God and Father of our Lord Jesus Christ, who hath blessed us with all Spiritual blessings in heavenly places in Christ:*" and for **Ephesians 2:5,** [God] "...*hath quickened us together with Christ...*" and in **verse 6**, "...*Hath raised us up together, and made us sit together in heavenly places in Christ Jesus."*
I declare grace, hope, charity, peace and love to abound in my life.
I loose the Anointing of God over me to fulfill all that you have planned for me; and for me to will and to do your good pleasure. Renew my mind, oh Lord, with your Word, so that I am well able to prove what is that good, acceptable, and perfect will of God for my life, as in **Romans 12:2**.
And in **Ephesians 3:16-19,** "*That He would grant you, according to the riches of His glory, to be strengthened with might by His Spirit in the inner man; That Christ may dwell in your hearts by faith; that ye, being rooted and grounded in love, may be able to comprehend with all saints what is the breadth, and length, and depth, and height; And to know the love of Christ, which passeth knowledge, that ye might be filled with all the fullness of God*".
I loose the Anointing of God over me to do as I'm instructed in Proverbs;   to   attend   and   keep   thy   Words,   Laws,   and

commandments. I ask you, God, to lead, guide and to direct me in all things. I ask for diligence, righteousness and to be a faithful ambassador who walks with wise men, with my soul and flesh full of abundant life, that life that you came, that I might have. I also ask, Lord, that you let me not be deceived. I loose the Anointing of God over me to be a counselor of peace and might with joy and a merry heart. I pray for my countenance to be youthful and cheerful, with a soft answer to turn away wrath; and for discretion, justice, equity, mercy, grace, truth, honor and riches to reign in my life.

I Loose the Anointing of God for my covenant rights to be dispatched unto me by the authority given me, in **Matthew 18:18, "Verily I say unto you, Whatsoever ye shall bind on earth shall be bound in heaven: and whatsoever ye shall loose on earth shall be loosed in heaven."** I loose the Anointing of God over me, that I may walk in the paths God prepared and hath before ordained for me to walk in; To bring forth all that He desires me to bring forth, for His glory- desires to fulfill His definite plans and His purposes for my life, and to show me how to pray most effectively, and to do all that He has commanded me to do. I put my all in your hands, Lord.

Proverbs 18:16, "A man's gift maketh room for him, and bringeth him before great men." I loose the Anointing of God over my gifts, and my talents. I ask for God's Anointing to make room for me before great men. I loose the Anointing of God over me for faith, mercy, grace, charity, peace, blessings, health, wealth, hope, praise, excellent spirits, discernment, comfort, contentment, love, power, a sound mind; and wholeness of soul, body, mind and spirit. I loose the Anointing of God over me for happiness, encouragement, honesty, trustworthiness, humility, and integrity.

I Loose the Anointing of God over me for the benefits of **Psalms 90:17, "And let the beauty of the Lord our God be upon us: and establish thou the work of our hands upon us; yea, the work of our hands establish thou it."** I thank you, Lord, that I have received of your fullness and your grace. **John 1:16** *"And of His fullness have all we received, and grace for grace."*

Galations 3:29, "And if ye be Christ's, then are ye Abraham's seed, and heirs according to the promise." As an heir of Abraham, I loose the Anointing of God for all the Abrahamic blessings and the favor of God and man to be poured out on each of us; and for the manifestation of the very best outcome of any, and all situations we encounter.

I thank you, God, that you make all grace abound toward me; that I, always, having all sufficiency in all things, may abound to every good work; I thank you that I'm the head and not the tail, that I'm above all and not beneath. I loose the Anointing of God over me for the full knowledge of my authority in you, Lord; I ask for full knowledge of how I rightfully use your Name, your Power, your Blood, your Spirit, your Authority and your Word for maximum benefit, and for me to be more than a conqueror through Christ who strengthens me.

II Corinthians 5:20, 21, I loose the Anointing of God over me to be an Ambassador for Christ, a soul winner and the righteousness of God in Christ.

I loose faith, hope and charity over me, **I Corinthians 13:13.**

I loose God's Anointing over me for restoration of life and nourishment; that God may retrieve, reverse and re-turn to the maximum all that I have lost.

I loose God's Anointing for a window of prophetic revelation to open, that I may know the plans for my prosperity and success. I loose God's Anointing over me for departure from strife, contention, and to receive, to inherit the promises that God has for me; all of the Abrahamic covenant promises. I loose God's Anointing for success in everything I do, great success in all that I do for God and for great success in all of my natural business. And, I ask for God to loose "the help" that He has prepared for me on my road ahead.

I sanctify myself and worship you, Lord, and loose your Anointing over me for positive generational connections and positive generational restoration.

Proverbs 19:23, *"The fear of the Lord tendeth to life: and he that hath it shall abide satisfied; he shall not be visited with evil."* I thank you, Lord, that you tendeth to my life because I fear you and I shall abide satisfied; and I shall not be visited with evil.

And, "...I will triumph in the works of thy hands," Psalms 92:4. ***"But thanks be to God, which giveth us the Victory through our Lord Jesus Christ,"*** I Corinthians 15:57.

Chapter Six – Sweet Hour of Prayer

I thank you, Father, that all things work together for my good, because I love you. **Romans 8:28,** *"And we know that all things work together for good to them that love God, to them who are the called according to His purpose."* *"Thou shalt increase my greatness, and comfort me on every side,"* **Psalms 71:21.** I give you praise, glory and honor, Lord; <u>I loose, declare and decree all of these things in the mighty name of Jesus.</u>

Church Leadership and God's Saints

I loose the Anointing of God over our pastors, every Christian minister, and saint around the world. I declare that we all abide in oneness, charity, love, strength, obedience, wisdom, revelation knowledge of the Word of God and in integrity. I declare that we all function in and move mightily in the gifts of the Spirit. And, that we all speak as oracles of God, boldly proclaiming the gospel, thoroughly equipped for the work of the ministry with the five-fold ministry operating in us.

I plead the blood of Jesus and loose the Anointing of God over each of us to be ambassadors for Christ, soul winners, and the righteousness of God in Christ. *" That He would grant you, according to the riches of His Glory, to be strengthened with might by His Spirit in the inner man; That Christ may dwell in your hearts by faith; that ye, being rooted and grounded in love, May be able to comprehend with all saints what is the breadth, and length, and depth, and height; And to know the love of Christ, which passeth knowledge, that ye might be filled with all the fullness of God,"* As we are admonished in **Ephesians 3:16-19.**

I thank you, God, that we are all *"...built upon the foundation of the apostles and the prophets, Jesus Christ Himself being the chief corner stone: In whom all the building fitly framed together groweth unto an holy temple in the Lord: In whom ye are also builded together for an habitation of God through the Spirit,"* according to **Ephesians 2:20-22.**

I plead the blood of Jesus upon the whole body of Christ and loose the anointing of God for all these benefits and for the manifestation of the divine provision of God over each, in Jesus' name.

Leaders of the U.S. and the World

I pray for and give thanks for all that are in authority, that we may lead a quiet and peaceable life, in all Godliness and honesty.

I loose the Anointing of God over our President, his cabinet, senate, all judges of our land and over all those in leadership in every state of our country. I loose the Anointing of God over the political hierarchy of the world that each leader will fulfill your calling upon their lives and your desires over their positions, politically and personally. I loose the Anointing of God to fill every political leadership position, from the top to the bottom, with righteous men and women, who will make sure that every law is based upon your standards. I declare safety and protection over all our service people and all our citizens on foreign soil.

I declare that there will be peace on earth and that your gospel is taken to the whole world, and all nations will worship you, for the Kingdom is yours and you are the governor among the nations, according to **Psalms 22:27, 28.** I thank you, Lord, that you rule and reign over all the earth and I give you praise.

Matthew 6:10, **"Thy Kingdom come, *Thy will be done in earth as it is in heaven."***

Prayer For The Lost

Psalms 2:8 *"Ask of me, and I shall give thee the heathen for thine inheritance, and the uttermost parts of the earth for thy possession;"* I ask for all lost souls to accept Jesus Christ as their Lord and Saviour. **II Corinthians 4:3, 4**, *"But if our gospel be hid, it is hid to them that are lost: In whom the god of this world hath blinded the minds of them which believe not, lest the light of the glorious gospel of Christ, who is the image of God, should shine unto them."*

I thank you, Lord, that the god of this world and the prince of the air is bound from the souls of the lost according to **Ephesians 2:2**, *"Wherein times past ye walked according to the course of this world, according to the prince of the power of the air, the spirit that now worketh in the children of disobedience:"*

I loose the Anointing of God over the minds of the lost to remove the mind blocks or blinds. I decree and declare that the light of God is shining on and around all of these that I place before you and I call them forth unto salvation. Please name the ones that you desire to be saved, now... We agree on their salvation in Jesus' name.

Loosening Physical and Spiritual Blessings

I loose the Anointing of God over my eyes according to **Ephesians 1:18,19.** *"The eyes of your understanding being enlightened; that ye may know what is the hope of His calling, and what the riches of the glory of His inheritance in the saints, and what is the exceeding greatness of His power to us-ward who believe, according to the working of His mighty power,"* **Saint Matthew** tells us in chapter **13**: verse **16**, *"But blessed are your eyes, for they see: and your ears, for they hear,"* I thank you, Lord, for restoration of my vision, spiritually and physically; for letting me see things as you do and for 20/20 Vision.

I loose the anointing of God over my ears and my lips, that I have attentive ears and an obedient heart to your voice, Lord. **Isaiah 50:** verses **4**, and **5** says, *"The Lord God hath given me the tongue of the learned, that I should know how to speak a word in season to him that is weary: He wakeneth morning by morning, HE WAKENETH MINE EAR TO HEAR AS THE LEARNED. THE LORD GOD HATH OPENED MINE EAR,"*

I declare my ears to hear as the learned, with the wisdom and knowledge of God; with great intelligence and for my lips to speak with meaningful eloquence; and that they speak only that which is pleasing in God's sight.

Psalms 141:3 *"Set a watch, O Lord, before my mouth; keep the door of my lips."* And in **I Peter 3:10**, *"For he that will love life, and see good days, let him refrain his tongue from evil, and his lips that they speak no guile."*

Philippians 2:5, *"Let this mind be in you, which was also in Christ Jesus:"*

Let me be always obedient to your will so that your same power that flowed through Jesus may flow through me today to bring your will to the earth.

I Loose the Anointing of God to transform my mind by aligning it with God's Word, which is God's will. **Romans 12:2** *"...but be ye transformed by the renewing of your mind, that ye may prove what is that good, and acceptable, and perfect will of God."* I loose the Anointing of God over me, that I might meditate day and night in your Word, so that I may observe to do according to all that is written therein: that I can make my way prosperous and have good success.

I declare that *"... I have the mind of Christ," I Corinthians 2:16,* and do hold the thoughts, feelings, and purposes of His heart. *"...But the Comforter, which is the Holy Ghost, whom the Father will send in my name, He shall teach you all things, and bring all things to your remembrance, whatsoever I have said unto you,"* John 14:26. I Loose the Power of the Holy Ghost within me to teach me all things and bring all things to my remembrance, whatsoever your Word says.

I declare that I have a photographic mind with instant recall, and full understanding of the Word of God and of all things that I desire to know; and the power to excell in all things, both written and oral. I loose the Anointing of God for Supernatural learning abilities and the wisdom and knowledge of God upon me. I decree that I have the tongue of the learned and that my ears hear as the learned, according to **Isaiah 50:4.** I loose the ability of God to declare the Word, to speak the Word in faith, to CO-CREATE WITH GOD, whatsoever I desire in Jesus' name.

I plead the blood of Jesus and loose the Anointing of God over my hands that they are diligent, creative and full of power. Whatever I put my hands to prospers, **Psalms 1:3,** and when I lay hands on the sick they recover, according to **Mark 16:18**.

I plead the blood of Jesus and loose the Anointing of God over my feet, that they stay on the pathway of righteousness; and that they are like hinds feet in high places, well able to overcome any obstacles of the enemy. My footsteps are directed and ordered by you, God, and my feet are beautiful because I deliver the gospel of peace and they are strong. **Deut. 33:25, *"Thy shoes shall be iron and brass; and as thy days, so shall thy strength be."***

I thank you, God, that my feet and legs are strong like iron and brass. My strength, also, is strong like iron and brass, and I walk in divine health all the days of my long life. I thank you, Lord, that I am physically strong.

I plead the blood of Jesus over my heart and loose the Anointing of the healing virtue of Jesus Christ over my heart, so that I am bold, stouthearted and inflexible to temptation. King David said in **Psalms 51:10,** *"Create in me a clean heart, oh God;"* And in **Ezekiel 36:26,** *"A new heart also will I give you, and a* *new Spirit will I put within you: and I will take away the stony heart out of your flesh, and I will give you an heart of flesh."* Joel 3:21, *"For I will cleanse their blood that I have not cleansed: for the Lord dwelleth in Zion."* I thank you, God, for total healing of my heart, my cardio-vascular system and every system of my body. I thank you for making me every way whole, both spiritually and physically.

"Bless the Lord, O my soul, and forget not all His benefits: Who forgiveth all thine iniquities; who healeth all thy diseases; Who redeemeth thy life from destruction; who crowneth thee with loving kindness and tender mercies; Who satisfieth thy mouth with good things; so that thy youth is renewed like the eagle's," Psalms 103:2-5.

"Be not wise in thine own eyes: fear the Lord, and depart from evil. It shall be health to thy navel (thy nerves)*, and marrow to thy bones,"* Proverbs 3:7, 8. I thank you, Lord, for a strong nervous system, healthy blood and a healthy skeletal system. I thank you that when I attend to thy Words, it is life unto me and health to all my flesh. **Proverbs 3:1, 2, *"My son, forget not my law; but let thine heart keep my commandments: For length of days, and long life, and peace, shall they add to thee."***

Proverbs 9:11, *"For by me thy days shall be multiplied, and the years of thy life shall be increased."*

"My son, attend to my Words; incline thine ear unto my sayings. Let them not depart from thine eyes; keep them in the midst of thine heart. For they are life unto those that find them, and health to all their flesh," **Proverbs 4:20-22.** And in **Isaiah 53:4, 5,** we are told, *"Surely He hath borne our griefs, and carried our sorrows: yet we did esteem Him stricken, smitten of God, and afflicted. But He was wounded for our transgressions, He was bruised for our iniquities: the chastisement of our peace was upon Him; and with His stripes we are healed."* After the cross, **I Peter 2:24** affirms, *"Who His own self bare our sins in His own body on the tree,that we, being dead to sins, should live unto righteousness: by whose stripes ye were healed."* I thank you, Jesus, for paying for the healing of our bodies over 2,000 years ago.

Romans 8:2,11, *"For the law of the Spirit of life in Christ*

Jesus hath made me free from the law of sin and death." "*But if the Spirit of Him that raised up Jesus from the dead dwell in you, He that raised up Christ from the dead shall also quicken your mortal bodies by His Spirit that dwelleth in you.*" I loose the Anointing of God and the Holy Ghost within me to quicken my mortal body to life abundant. **Psalms 118:17,** "*I shall not die, but live, and declare the works of the Lord.*"

   JOB 21:23,24, I thank you, that I will die in my full strength, being wholly at ease and quiet, completely secure, my body well nourished and my bones rich with marrow.

   I plead the blood of Jesus and loose the Anointing of the healing virtue of Jesus Christ over me from top to bottom, throughout every system of my body. Throughout every major and minor organ; including every cell, and fiber of my being for the perfect functioning of each of my body systems. I loose the Anointing of God over my entire body for complete normality, for total healing, that I may walk in divine health all the days of my long life. I claim, declare, and decree all these things in the name and in the Blood of Jesus Christ.

Protection

Isaiah 54:17, *"No weapon that is formed against thee shall prosper;* and every tongue that shall rise against thee in judgment thou shalt condemn. This is the heritage of the servants of the Lord, and their righteousness is of me, saith the Lord."

Psalms 37:39, 40, "But the salvation of the righteous is of the Lord: He is their strength in time of trouble. And the Lord shall help them, and deliver them: He shall deliver them from the wicked, and save them, because they trust in Him."

Deuteronomy 33:26,27,29, "There is none like unto the God of Jeshurun, (God's chosen) who rideth upon the heaven in thy help and in His excellency on the sky. The eternal God is thy refuge, and underneath are the everlasting arms: and He shall thrust out the enemy from before thee; and shall say, Destroy them." " Happy art thou, O Israel: who is like unto thee, O people saved by the Lord, the shield of thy help, and who is the sword of thy excellency! And thine enemies shall be found liars unto thee; and thou shalt tread upon their high places." I thank you, God, that in **Isaiah 54:14**, we're told, *"In righteousness shalt thou be established: thou shalt be far from oppression; for thou shalt not fear: and from terror; for it shall not come near thee."*

Psalms 91:10, *"There shall no evil befall thee, neither shall any plague come nigh thy dwelling."*

Psalms 7:10, *"My defense is of God, which saveth the upright in heart."*

Psalms 16:5, *"The Lord is the portion of mine inheritance and of my cup: thou maintainest my lot."* (He guards all that is mine.)

Psalms 25:10, *"All the paths of the Lord are mercy and truth unto such as keep His covenant and His testimonies."*

Psalms 91:11,12, *"For he shall give His angels charge over thee, to keep thee in all thy ways. They shall bear thee up in their hands, lest thou dash thy foot against a stone."*

II Timothy 4:18, *"AND THE LORD SHALL DELIVER ME FROM EVERY EVIL WORK, AND WILL PRESERVE ME UNTO HIS HEAVENLY KINGDOM:"*

 I loose the Power in all of these scriptures and the Anointing of the protection of God Almighty over my spouse, children, family, Pastors and myself; I loose God's protection over each one for which I pray, our families, businesses, occupations, properties, and possessions in the name and in the blood of Jesus Christ.

You will find more Protection Scriptures under Chapter Twenty.

Chapter Six – Sweet Hour of Prayer

LOOSENING FINANCIAL BLESSINGS

Psalms 65:11, *"Thou crownest the year with thy goodness; and thy paths drop fatness,"* (you drop your bounty in my paths.)

Psalms 94:14, *"For the Lord will not cast off his people, neither will He forsake his inheritance."*

Isaiah 45:2, 3, *"I will go before thee, and make the crooked places straight: I will break in pieces the gates of brass, and cut in sunder the bars of iron: And I will give thee the treasures of darkness, and hidden riches of secret places, that thou mayest know that I, the Lord, which call thee by thy name, am the God of Israel."*

Psalms 71:21, "Thou shalt increase my greatness, and comfort me on every side."

Proverbs 15:6, *"In the house of the righteous is much treasure: But in the revenues of the wicked is trouble."*

Proverbs 22:4, *"By humility and the fear of the Lord are Riches, and Honor, and Life."*

Job 22:24, 25, *"Then shalt thou lay up gold as dust, and the gold of O'phir as the stones of the brooks. Yea, the Almighty shall be thy defense, and thou shalt have plenty of silver."*

Psalms 23:5, *"...my cup runneth over."*

Proverbs 8:21, "That I may cause those that love me to inherit substance; and I will fill their treasures."

Psalms 35:27, *"Let them shout for joy, and be glad, that favor my righteous cause: yea, let them say continually, Let the Lord be magnified, which hath pleasure in the prosperity of His servant."*

I thank you, Lord, that you make all grace abound toward me; that I, always having all sufficiency in all things, may abound to every good work: As it is written, he hath dispersed abroad, he hath given to the poor, his righteousness remaineth forever.

Lord, *"Both riches and honour come of thee, and thou reignest over all; and in thine hand is power and might; and in thine hand it is to make great, and to give strength unto all. Now therefore, our God, we thank thee, and praise thy glorious name."*
I Chronicles 29:12, 13. My soul and my seeds souls shall dwell at

ease, inherit the earth and abide in prosperity because we fear you Lord, as in **Psalms 25:12,13.**

"The Lord shall increase you more and more, you and your children," **Psalms 115:14.** *"The secret of the Lord is with them that fear Him and He will shew them His covenant,"* **Psalms 25:14.**

I thank you, *"For thou Lord, hast made me glad through thy work: I will triumph in the works of thy hands,"* **Psalms 92:4.** *"Because I fear you oh Lord you tendeth to my life; and I abide satisfied* (in great prosperity), *and I shall not be visited with evil,"* *"The blessing of the Lord, it maketh rich, and He addeth no sorrow with it."* **Proverbs 10:22**.

I declare that I have the Power, the ability and the Anointing of God to get wealth to establish His covenant, the covenant that He cut with Abraham. The same covenant that He promised to Isaac, Jacob, and his seed, myself and my seed; because we are heirs according to that Promise. I am a covenant partner with God and I am blessed. I am on my way to wealthy places: God gave us a promise and He never lies.

I declare that it is time now, for the manifestation of all my covenant promises and all my desires. **Psalms 118:25,** *"Save now, I beseech thee, O Lord: Oh Lord, I beseech thee, send now prosperity."*

I claim my breakthrough now, in Jesus' name. I decree, and loose God's Anointing upon me for Supernatural Power to get wealth; Empowerment through dreams, visions, ideas, wisdom, and inventions. I plead the Blood of Jesus and loose the Anointing of God over me, for Supernatural Power to fulfill all my covenant promises for prosperity in all things and for the provision of all my needs and desires. I loose the Anointing of God for an exponential multiplication of all my good seed sown and total crop failure of any bad seed sown. I declare and decree, that I have Supernatural wealth and prosperity in all things. I loose the Anointing of God over me, for total fulfillment of all these things, for your glory and your honor, Lord, in Jesus' Name. Amen!

FAITH IN GOD'S WORD

Hebrews 10:21-23, *"And having a high priest over the house of God; Let us draw near with a true heart in full assurance of faith, having our hearts sprinkled from an evil conscience, and our bodies washed with pure water. Let us hold fast the profession of our faith without wavering; (for He is faithful that promised;)"*

Hebrews 4:2, *"For unto us was the gospel* (The Word) *preached, as well as unto them: but the Word preached did not profit them, NOT BEING MIXED WITH FAITH in them that heard it."*

Romans 1:16, *"For I am not ashamed of the gospel* (the Word) *of Christ: for it is the power of God…"*.

Hebrews 11:1, *"Now Faith is the substance of things hoped for, the evidence of things not seen."* I thank you, Lord, that even now, faith is giving substance (a foundation) to things I am hoping for and bringing evidence (the manifestation) to things I can't yet see.

Philippians 4:9 *"Those things, which ye have both learned, and received, and heard, and seen in me, do: and the God of peace shall be with you."* And in **Genesis 1:3,** We see God framing, building His world, showing us how He did it, **And in the seven days of creation GOD SAID WORDS! God called everything into existence. And in v. 31,** *"GOD SAW!"* God saw everything that He had made, and behold it was very good. The Lord's Words are Spirit and life. I thank you Father, that you made the world and all things in it, with your Words.

Jesus praying to our Father in **John 17:8** said, *"For I have given unto them the Words which thou gavest me,"* and in **John 17:13,14,17,** Jesus, still in prayer, said, *"And now I come to thee; and these things I speak in the world, that they might have my joy fulfilled in themselves. I have given them thy WORD;"* *"Sanctify them through thy truth: thy Word is truth."*

I thank you, Lord, that you came to earth and showed us how to speak your Word and told us to speak your Word out of our mouths. **Matthew 4:4,** Jesus told the devil, *"It is written, Man* shall not live by bread alone, but by every Word that proceedeth out of the mouth of God." <u>The Word is called the living Bible because it is alive.</u>

Hebrews 4:12, *"For The Word of God is quick* (alive) *and powerful...."*

Hebrews 1:2, 3 (God), *"... Hath in these last days spoken unto us by His Son, whom He hath appointed heir of all things, by whom also He made the worlds; Who being the brightness of His glory, and the express image of His person, and upholding all things by the Word of His power, when He had by Himself purged our sins, sat down on the right hand of the Majesty on high;"*

Hebrews 11:3, *"Through faith we understand that the worlds were framed by the Word of God, so that things which are seen were not made of things which do appear."* <u>When I speak God's Word in faith, believing and doubting not, the Lord, who upholdeth all things by the WORD of HIS POWER, uses FAITH SUBSTANCE to create that which I call forth; GOD used faith substance to create all things; our bodies and everything that was made.</u>   In **John 1:3,** we find that, *"All things were made by Him; and without Him was not anything made that was made."*

And in **Isaiah 44:24, 26**, *"Thus saith the Lord, thy redeemer, and He that formed thee from the womb, I am the Lord that maketh all things; that stretcheth forth the heavens alone; that spreadeth abroad the earth by myself;" "... That confirmeth the Word of His servant, and performeth the counsel of His messengers."*

<u>Your Word which I speak, Lord, is my confirmation, my guarantee of the things for which I am believing</u>. **Mark 16: 20**, *"And they went forth, and preached everywhere, the Lord working with them, and confirming the Word with signs following. Amen."*

"Ask, and it shall be given you; seek, and ye shall find; knock, and it shall be opened unto you: For every one that asketh receiveth; and he that seeketh findeth; and to him that knocketh it shall be opened." **Matthew 7:7,8.**

"Delight thy self also in the Lord; and He shall give thee the desires of thine heart. Commit thy way unto the Lord; trust also in Him; and He shall bring it to pass." **Psalms 37:4, 5.**

I have faith in God! I say unto this mountain, be thou removed, and be thou cast into the sea; and I shall not doubt in my heart, but I shall believe that those things, which I say, shall come to pass; I shall have whatsoever I say. I believe that I receive all the requests that I ask for and I declare that God will see to it that I shall have them, as we are told in **Mark 11:22, 23, 24.** I thank you, Father God, for your promise in **Psalms 89:34**, *"My covenant will I not break, nor alter the thing that is gone out of my lips."*

Jeremiah 1:12, *"Then said the Lord unto me, thou hast well seen: for I will hasten* (hurry, speed-up) *my Word to perform it."* I thank you, God, that the things which are impossible with men, are possible with you, **Luke 18:27.**

I have faith as a grain of mustard seed and I shall say unto this mountain (of impossibilities)," Remove hence to yonder place!", and it shall remove; and nothing shall be impossible unto me, **Matthew 17:20.** And in **Mark 9:23** Jesus said unto him, *"...If thou canst believe, all things are possible to him that believeth."* And we find in **1 John 5:14,15,** *"And this is the confidence that we have in Him, that, if we ask any thing according to His will, He heareth us: And if we know that He heareth us, whatsoever we ask, we know that we have the petitions that we desired of Him."*

Psalms 20:1-5 *"The Lord hear thee in the day of trouble; the name of the God of Jacob defend thee; Send thee help from the sanctuary, and strengthen thee out of Zion; Remember all thy offerings, and accept thy burnt sacrifice; Selah. Grant thee according to thine own heart, and fulfill all thy counsel. We will rejoice in thy salvation, and in the name of our God we will set up our banners: the Lord fulfill all thy petitions."*

The LORD IS FULFILLING ALL OF MY PETITIONS! All the forces of heaven are backing me up, because I am a child of the Most High God. I decree that I am walking in the authority that my Father has given me; God is backing me up - El Shaddi - The God of more than enough! The same power that raised Christ from the dead dwells within me. I won't consider the circumstances, I will consider God! *"I can do all things through Christ which strengtheneth me,"* **Philippians 4:13.** And we find in **Romans 8:31,32,37,** *"... If God be for us, who can be against us? He*

that spared not his own Son, but delivered Him up for us all,
how shall He not with Him also freely give us all things?"
   " Nay, in all these things we are more than conquerors
through Him that loved us." The Word tells us in **Acts 27:25**,
"Wherefore, sirs, be of good cheer: for I believe God that it
shall be even as it was told me."
   I declare and decree that all of God's promises to me are true
and are being manifested to me now, according to His Word,
because I keep His commandments. His Word is faith filled; it is
truth, light, quick, alive, and powerful. I speak His Word with my
mouth, mix His faith filled words with my faith, and it is bringing
forth all of my decrees, hopes, desires, and dreams. The Word is
bringing forth the favor of God and man; and the manifestation of
all that I have asked for, because The WORD is GOD!
   My words, which are based on God's Word, are self-fulfilling
prophecies which are shaping my world. God's promises, my
covenant blessings that I call forth, are bringing me a prosperous,
healthy future. I loose the Anointing of God over me for all positive
ancestral, generational inheritances, orphan seeds and blessings
to descend upon me, and my children. I am moving quickly into an
unending season of manifestation of perfect health, exponential
wealth and a great future. I declare an unending season full of
God's richest blessings with treasures abundant, because I am a
child of the King and I declare that Supernatural Signs will follow
me all the days of my long life!
   God is my source. I am in alignment with God's Word and I
expect God's best over my life, my future, everything I do and over
all of my finances. I AM FILLED WITH "CAN DO" POWER, "CAN
DO" WORDS, GOD'S WORDS AND VICTORIOUS ANSWERS! I
AM VICTORIOUS IN ALL THINGS! I have a perpetual, dynamic
relationship with God Almighty and I continually defeat Satan and
all evil. The forces of evil see the BLOOD of JESUS over me and
all for whom I pray, over all of our businesses, properties and
possessions: I walk in the authority of God and keep the BLOOD
OF JESUS over me continually; therefore, the enemy is under my
feet!
   Romans 4:16-18, *"Therefore it is of faith, that it might be*
by grace; to the end the promise might be sure to all the
seed;" "... even God, who quickeneth the dead, and calleth

those things that be not as though they were." And (Abraham), *"Who against hope believed in hope, that he might become the father of many nations, according to that which was spoken, So shall thy seed be."*

I declare **Romans 8:38, 39,** over me and over all for whom I pray: *"For I am persuaded, that neither death, nor life, nor angels, nor principalities, nor powers, nor things present, nor things to come, Nor height, nor depth, nor any other creature, shall be able to separate us from the love of God, which is in Christ Jesus our Lord."*

CONCLUSION

I loose the Anointing of God over me for an exponential multiplication of my good seed sown and a mighty increase in the fruits of my righteousness. I loose the Anointing of God over me, for enrichment in everything to all bountifulness and I am thankful to you, Father, for everything. I loose the Anointing of God over me for great faith, because **Romans 14:23** says, *"For whatsoever is not of faith is sin."*

"Now I know that the Lord saveth His anointed; He will hear me from His holy heaven with the saving strength of His right hand," **Psalms 20:6.**

"Now unto Him that is able to do exceeding abundantly above all that we ask or think, according to the power that worketh in us, Unto Him be glory in the church by Jesus Christ through out all ages, world without end." **Ephesians 3: 20,21.** *"... For thine is the Kingdom, and the power, and the glory, for ever. Amen"* **Matthew 6:13.**

I have given voice to my covenant, your Word, Father and I loose the power and the Anointing of God, to bind unto me all of these wonderful blessings, all of my covenant promises. I thank you, God, that you watch over your Word to perform it. I loose the power of my guardian, bidding, ministering angels and the angels of the Lord, to establish these decrees, declarations, this earnest petition and to bring all this good to me for your glory, Lord. I bind all the Abrahamic covenant blessings, and all these benefits unto me, and I give thanks unto God in the name of our Lord, Jesus Christ. *"... be it done unto me according to thy Word",* as Mary said to the angel in **Luke 1:38**. It is established, in Jesus' name. Amen, Amen, Amen.

Jeremiah 15:16, *"Thy words were found, and I did eat them; and thy Word was unto me the joy and rejoicing of my heart: for I am called by thy name, O Lord God of hosts."* I thank you, Father, for all of your Word and for all of these covenant blessings.

"Giving thanks always for all things unto God and the Father in the name of our Lord Jesus Christ;" **Ephesians 5:20.**

"Now unto him that is able to keep you from falling, and to present you faultless before the presence of His glory with exceeding joy, To the only wise God our Saviour, be glory and majesty, dominion and power, both now and ever." Jude 1:24, 25.

John 3:22 *"And whatsoever we ask, we receive of Him, because we keep His commandments, and do those things that are pleasing in His sight."*

<u>NOTES</u>

Daily Prayer -Twenty-Minute
Introduction

These prayers are based on the Word of God, according to the outline given in the Lord's Prayer. Before we begin our daily prayer, let us prepare our hearts to come before our God.

You must connect with God; stir up the Holy Ghost within you, in order to have a dynamic prayer. You must have a heart connection with God Almighty, and you must pray the Word in earnest, to pray effectively. So empty your mind of the cares of the world; Let go of all your worries and concentrate on and meditate on the Word, as we pray our daily prayer.

The Word is mighty and it is powerful, and the Word is God! When you meditate on the Word and pray it from your heart, it is not just a form and it assures you of having the attention of, and the ear of God. God watches over His Word to perform it. Earnestly pray along with me, and expect your harvest. His promises to us are all yes, and amen, in Christ Jesus.

Follow along with me as the angels of the Lord establish our words, which are based on God's Word.

Putting on the Armor of God

I put on the whole armor of God of **Ephesians 6:11-18, that** I may be able to stand against the wiles of the devil. I put on the breastplate of righteousness, the helmet of salvation. My loins are gird about with truth, my feet shod with the preparation of the gospel of peace. I take the shield of faith, to quench the fiery darts of the wicked, and the sword of the Spirit, the Word of God, to defeat Satan on every hand. **Ephesians 6:19,** *"And for me, that utterance may be given unto me, that I may open my mouth boldly, to make known the mystery of the gospel, For which I am an ambassador in bonds:" "...and having done all, to stand!"* **Ephesians 6:13.**

I plead the blood of Jesus over me, from the top of my head to the soles of my feet, and throughout every system and cell of my being. I ask you, Lord, to place this same armor and blood protection on and around my spouse, children, pastors, and family members, and everything I bind and loose, I do also for each of them, in Jesus' name.

I thank you, God, that we overcome Satan by the blood of the Lamb and by the word of our testimony, Amen.

Binding Satan and
Reversing all Curses

Thus saith the Lord God, in **Matthew 18:18,** *"Verily I say unto you, Whatsoever ye shall bind on earth shall be bound in heaven: and whatsoever ye shall loose on earth shall be loosed in heaven."*

I address, rebuke, and bind you Satan, all fallen angels, evil spirits - principalities, powers, rulers of the darkness of this world, spiritual wickedness in high places and every evil spirit and power that you rule, command and have jurisdiction over, including the prince of the air; And I cast everyone of you into outer darkness, in Jesus' name.

I bind and cast into the sea every evil assignment from every evil source, their causes and effects on all levels, spiritually, physically, emotionally, financially and socially. I bind all evil spirits and all evil assignments from my spouse, children, pastors, myself and our family members, and cast them all into the sea, in Jesus' name, according to **Mark 11:23**. Thus saith the Lord, *"For verily I say unto you, that whosoever shall say unto this mountain, be thou removed, and be thou cast into the sea; and shall not doubt in his heart, but shall believe that those things which he saith shall come to pass; he shall have whatsoever he saith."*

I loose the Anointing of God and the power of **Isaiah 10:27,** to destroy the yolk of evil. I confess our bodies are temples of the Holy Ghost, redeemed, sanctified, cleansed, blood bought and justified by the Blood of Jesus.

I BREAK AND REVERSE ALL CURSES AGAINST EACH OF US. I THANK YOU, LORD, FOR SETTING US FREE, IN JESUS' NAME. AMEN.

Colossians 2:13-15, *"And you, being dead in your sins and the uncircumcision of your flesh, hath He quickened together with him, having forgiven you all trespasses; Blotting out the handwriting of ordinances that was against us, which was contrary to us, and took it out of the way, nailing it to His cross; And having spoiled principalities and powers, He made a shew of them openly, triumphing over them in it."*

Colossians 2:10, *"And ye are complete in Him, which is the head of all principality and power:"*

Romans 8:2, *"For the Law of the Spirit of life in Christ Jesus hath made me free from the law of sin and death."*

<u>NOTES</u>

Daily Prayer-Twenty Minute

Our Dear Heavenly Father, I boldly come into your gates with thanksgiving and into your courts with praise, by the Blood of Jesus that gives me that right and authority. I thank you, Lord, for your love, mercy, grace, peace and for all of your blessings unto me and my family. I thank you for the Anointing of the Holy Ghost; I thank you for everything.

I ask Jesus, my Chief High Priest, to plead my declarations together with me before you, that I may be justified, according to **Isaiah 43:26.** *"Put me in remembrance: let us plead together; declare thou, that thou mayest be justified."*

Psalms 4:3, *"But know that the Lord hath set apart him that is Godly for Himself: the Lord will hear when I call unto Him."*

I seek first the Kingdom of God and your righteousness. Everything I pray for myself, I pray for my spouse, my children, pastors and family members.

I declare that I serve the King of Kings, the Lord of Lords, the Lord of hosts. You are my Redeemer, my Shepherd, the Light of the world, the Alpha and the Omega, the Maker and Ruler of all, and beside you there is no other. You are my Faithful God, Holy and Just, my Rock, my Shelter, my Strong Tower, my Deliverer, and I rejoice in you. You are my strength, my Savior, and Hallowed is thy name, which I exalt, honor, glorify, magnify, praise and worship. I rejoice and give thanks that you are my All, in All.

John 1:1 *"In the beginning was the Word, and the Word was with God, and the Word was God."* I thank you, Father, that I can speak your faith filled Words, mix your Words with my faith, and mountains have to move when I command them. I thank you that we can co-create with you according to **Mark 11:23, 24, 25.**

I thank you, Father, for heaven and I rejoice because my name is written in the Lambs' book of life, **Luke 10:20.** I declare that I will be glad in this day that you have made, **Psalms 118:24.**

I thank you, Father, that you have given the earth and the authority to dominate the earth to the children of men. In **Genesis 1:26** God said, *"... Let them have dominion over...all the earth."* I plead the blood of Jesus, declare and loose the Anointing of God for the protection and safety of America, Jerusalem, Israel, our president, our military and every American citizen throughout the world.

I ask, Lord, that you send forth laborers for the harvest. I declare peace, justice and the truth of God's Kingdom to be realized in each country, as it is in heaven. I declare that you rule and reign over all the earth, and you are Lord over all.

I repent before you, Lord, and ask forgiveness for anything that I've done, said or thought, unpleasing in your sight. I forgive others of their debts and offenses unto me, that I may be forgiven. **James 4:8,** tells us to draw nigh to God and He will draw nigh unto us. I dedicate and consecrate my life unto you. I seek your face, your purposes and desires for my life. Help me to trust always in you, with all of my heart, mind, soul and strength. Help me to acknowledge you in all my ways so that you will direct my paths; to fear you, and to forever depart from evil, as we are told in **Proverbs 3:5-7.** I ask Lord that you, *"Order my steps in thy Word: and let not any iniquity have dominion over me. Deliver me from the oppression of man: so will I keep thy precepts."* **Psalms 119:133, 134.**

I loose the Anointing of God over me for protection from temptation and deliverance from all evil; and for travel mercies and travel grace. I declare that no weapon formed against me shall prosper and every thing I do, shall prosper: *"But the salvation of the righteous is of the Lord: He is their strength in time of trouble. And the Lord shall help them, and deliver them: He shall deliver them from the wicked, and save them, because they trust in Him,"* **Psalms 37:39, 40.** And in **Psalms 91:10-12** we are told, *"There shall no evil befall thee, neither shall any plague come nigh thy dwelling. For He shall give His angels charge over thee, to keep thee in all thy ways. They shall bear thee up in their hands, lest thou dash thy foot against a stone."*

I declare the promises of the **Twenty-Third Psalms**, and the benefits of **Psalms 46:1, 2,** over each of us. "*God is our refuge and strength, a very present help in trouble. Therefore will not we fear, though the earth be removed, and though the mountains be carried into the midst of the sea."*

I loose the Anointing of God over every Christian pastor,

minister, prayer warrior, musician, singer and saint around the world. I declare that we all abide in oneness, charity, love, strength, obedience, wisdom, revelation knowledge of the Word of God and in integrity. I declare that we all function in, and move mightily in, the gifts of the Spirit -that we all speak as oracles of God, boldly proclaiming the gospel, thoroughly equipped for the work of the ministry with the five-fold ministry operating in us. I ask that you show us great and mighty things. I plead the blood of Jesus and loose the Anointing of God over each of us, to be ambassadors for Christ, soul winners, the righteousness of God in Christ and for all these benefits, and the divine provision of God to be loosed over each of us, in Jesus' name.

"That He would Grant you, according to the riches of His Glory, to be strengthened with might by His Spirit in the inner man; That Christ may dwell in your hearts by faith; that ye, being rooted, and grounded in love, may be able to comprehend with all saints what is the breadth, and length, and depth, and height: And to know the love of Christ, which passeth knowledge, that ye might be filled with all the fullness of God," *as in* **Ephesians 3:16-19.**

II Corinthians 4:3, 4, "*But if our gospel be hid, it is hid to them that are lost: In whom the god of this world hath blinded the minds of them which believe not, lest the light of the glorious gospel of Christ, who is the image of God, should shine unto them.*"

I thank you, God, that the prince of the air is bound from the souls of the lost. I loose the Anointing of God over all the lost, to remove the mind blocks. I declare the light of the glorious gospel of Christ, the image of God, shining on and around, all these that I place before you and I call them unto salvation. Please name the ones that you desire to be saved, now.........We agree on their salvation in Jesus' name.

As in II Corinthians 10:4,5, I loose unto me mighty weapons of warfare through God to the pulling down of strong holds: Casting down imaginations and every high thing that exalteth itself against the knowledge of God, and bringing into captivity, every thought to the obedience of Christ; And declare that, I have the mind of Christ **I Corinthians 2:16**, and do hold the thoughts, feelings and purposes of His heart.

"But the Comforter, which is the Holy Ghost, whom the Father will send in my name, He shall teach you all things, and bring all things to your remembrance, whatsoever I have said unto you." John14: 26.

I loose the Anointing of God for a photographic memory, instant recall and full understanding of the Word of God and all desirable things, and the power to excel in each. I loose miraculous supernatural learning abilities, and the wisdom and knowledge of God, strong character, and open doors to complete success in all things. I declare that I have a teachable spirit, the tongue of the learned and that my ears hear, according to **Isaiah 50:4**. I loose the ability of God within me to speak God's Words, God's blessings, and covenant promises over my life. God's Words are Spirit and life, and they created all things. I declare the Word in faith, to co-create with God whatsoever I desire, in Jesus' name.

I loose the Anointing of God to impart unto me the manifestation of the gifts of the Spirit, according to I **Corinthians 12:7-11.** I ask that God impart unto me the word of wisdom, the word of knowledge, faith, the gifts of healing, the working of miracles, prophecy, discernment of spirits, tongues and interpretations, dividing unto me severally as you will Lord, that I may profit with all. I declare that all the gifts of the Spirit are operating in my life. I am a soul winner, I'm bold for Christ, faithful and steadfast in the Lord, and I use my talents and gifts to glorify you, Lord.

I plead the blood of Jesus; and loose the anointing of the healing virtue of Jesus Christ over me from top to bottom, throughout every system of my body, throughout every major and minor organ, every cell and fiber of my being; for the perfect functioning of each of my body systems, for total healing. I loose the Anointing of God over me for restoration of life and nourishment. I declare that I am happy, strong, and I walk in divine health all the days of my long life. I can do all things through Christ who strengthens me and who always gives me peace, security, riches and honor. Victory in all things is mine, my whole life through and I will triumph over all opposition because it is my heritage as a child of God.

I declare that I have the power, the ability, and the Anointing of God to get wealth to establish God's covenant. To establish the same covenant He cut with Abraham, promised to Isaac, Jacob and his seed, myself and my seed, because we are heirs according to that promise. I claim the laws of restitution to be operational in my life, that God may retrieve, reverse, and re-turn to the maximum, all that I've lost.

I declare a window of prophetic revelation to open and plans for my success and prosperity to unfold. I use my talents and gifts to glorify you, Lord. I receive what I ask for, and find that for which I am looking. I am a covenant partner with God and I am blessed.

I declare that I live under an open heaven. God is the director of my path; and I will fulfill the calling, and destiny that God has planned for me. I decree the favor of God over my communications, relationships, and travels. I declare, that our home is as the days of heaven on earth, **Deut.11:18-21,** because I love you, Lord, and I keep your commandments.

I loose God's Anointing upon me for Supernatural power to get wealth: empowerment through dreams, visions, ideas, wisdom and inventions. I declare and decree, I plead the blood of Jesus, and loose the Anointing of God, for signs and wonders, many miracles, and the fulfillment of every covenant promise for prosperity in my life. I declare that I live under an open heaven, and decree an exponential multiplication of all my good seed sown, and total crop failure, of any bad seed sown.

I decree all of God's promises to me are true and are being manifested to me now through Christ Jesus because I keep His commandments. My words, which are based on God's Word, are self-fulfilling prophecies that are shaping my world. I thank you, God, that I will always walk in my covenant rights, in excess, in overflow, in the divine provision of God, the director of my path.

I loose the Anointing of God for all positive ancestral, generational inheritances and blessings to ascend upon me and my children. I am a Supernatural person and I am now moving into an unending season of miracle manifestations of perfect health, exponential wealth and a great future filled with wonderful people: an unending season full of God's richest blessings, with open doors and treasures abundant, because I am a child of The King. I declare and decree that God is increasing my territory and Supernatural signs of prosperity, in all things, will follow me all the days of my long life.

You are my source God, I am in alignment with your Word and I expect your best over my life. I am fully persuaded that the extreme favor of God and man is over my life, my children, my finances, my possessions, my future, and everything that I do. I am filled with the creative ability of God; I am filled with "Can Do" words, God's Words, and I am victorious in all things! My life demonstrates the will, the power, and the love of God. **Romans 4:21, "And being fully persuaded that, what He had promised, He was able also to perform."**

I have given voice to my covenant, your Word, Father, and I loose the power and the Anointing of God, to bind unto me all of these wonderful blessings, all of my covenant promises. I thank you, Father, that you watch over your Word to perform it. I loose the power of my guardian, bidding, ministering angels and the angels of the Lord to establish these decrees, declarations, this earnest petition; and to bring all of this good to me, for your glory, Lord. I bind all the Abrahamic covenant blessings, and all of these benefits to me, and I give thanks unto God, in the name of our Lord Jesus Christ. **"... be it unto me according to thy Word,"** as Mary said to the angel, in **Luke 1:38**. It is established in Jesus' name. Amen.

Revelations 5:13, "...Blessing, and honor, and glory, and power, be unto Him that sitteth upon the throne, and unto the Lamb, for ever and ever." Amen.

Daily Prayer-Ten Minute
Introduction

These prayers are based on the Word of God, according to the outline given in the Lord's Prayer. Before we begin our daily prayer, let us prepare our hearts to come before our God, put on the whole armor of God, our blood protection, and bind Satan and all evil according to **Matthew 18:18,** in Jesus' name.

You must connect with God; stir up the Holy Ghost within you, in order to have a dynamic prayer. You must have a heart connection with God almighty, and you must pray the Word in earnest, to pray effectively. So empty your mind of the cares of the world, let go of all your worries, and concentrate on, meditate on, the Lord, as we pray our daily prayer.

The Word is mighty, and it is powerful and the Word is God! When you meditate on the Word, and pray it from your heart. It is not just a form and it assures you of having the attention of and the ear of God. God watches over His Word to perform it. Earnestly pray along with me and expect your harvest. His promises to us are all "Yes", and "Amen", in Christ Jesus.

Follow along with me as the angels of God establish our words which are based on God's Word.

Putting on the Armor of God

I put on the whole armor of God that I may be able to stand against the attacks of the devil. I put on the breastplate of righteousness, the helmet of salvation, my loins are gird about with truth, and my feet are shod, with the preparation of the gospel of peace. I take the shield of faith, to quench the fiery darts of the wicked, and the sword of the Spirit, the Word of God, to defeat Satan on every hand.

I plead the blood of Jesus over me from the top of my head to the bottom of my feet, and throughout every system and cell of my being, for protection from all evil. I ask you Lord, to place this same armor, and this same blood protection on and around my spouse, children, pastors, and family members, and everything I pray, bind and loose for myself, I also do for each of these, in Jesus' name, Amen.

Binding Satan and all Evil

I address, rebuke, and bind Satan, all evil principalities, powers, rulers of the darkness of this world, spiritual wickedness in high places, the prince of the air and every demonic spirit and power that you rule, command, and have jurisdiction over, and cast you all into outer darkness.

I bind and cast into the sea, every evil assignment, their causes and effects against us on all levels, spiritually, physically, emotionally, financially and socially, and I break and reverse all curses against us, in Jesus' name.

I confess that our bodies are temples of the Holy Ghost, redeemed, sanctified, cleansed, blood bought, and justified by the Blood of Jesus Christ, and I declare that Satan is under our feet .I thank you Lord, for setting us free, in Jesus' name. Amen.

Daily Prayer - Ten Minute

Our Dear Heavenly Father, I come into your gates with thanksgiving and into your courts with praise, by the Blood of Jesus, that gives me that right and authority. I thank you, Father, for everything, and I ask Jesus, my Chief High Priest, to plead my declarations together with me before you, that I may be justified. I seek first the Kingdom of God, and your Righteousness. Everything I declare, ask for, and pray for myself, I also pray for my spouse, children, pastors, and family members.

I declare that I serve the King of Kings, and the Lord of Lords. Holy Father, you are my Redeemer, my Shepherd, my Strong Tower, my Deliverer, and Hallowed is thy name. I worship and praise you, Lord. You are my All, in All.

I thank you, God, for our wonderful promise of heaven, and I rejoice because my name is written in the Lamb's book of life! I declare that I will be glad in this wonderful day that you have made, and I'm thankful that your mercies are new every morning.

I plead the blood of Jesus, declare, and loose the Anointing of God over America, our president, Jerusalem, Israel, our military, and our citizens, in every country of the world. I ask for peace, justice and the truth of God's Kingdom to be realized in each country, as it is in heaven. I ask that you send forth laborers into your harvest. I declare that you rule and reign over all the earth, and you are Lord over all.

I repent before you, Lord, and ask forgiveness of anything that I've done, said or thought, unpleasing in your sight. I forgive others easily and I love all people.

I loose the Anointing of God over me for protection from temptation and deliverance from all evil. I loose the anointing of God over me for travel protection, travel mercies and travel grace. I declare that no weapon formed against me shall prosper, and everything I do shall prosper. There shall no evil befall me, neither shall any plague come nigh my dwelling. God's angels have charge over me, to keep me in all my ways. They bear me up in their hands, lest I dash my foot against a stone.

I loose the Anointing of God, and plead the blood of Jesus, over every Christian pastor, minister, prayer warrior, musician, singer, and the whole body of Christ around the world. I declare that we all function in, and move mightily in the gifts of the Spirit, speaking as oracles of God, boldly proclaiming the gospel, thoroughly equipped with the five-fold ministry operating in us. I ask, Lord, that you show us great and mighty things. We are ambassadors for Christ, soul winners, and the righteousness of God through Christ. I declare all of these benefits, and the complete provision of God for all things, over each.

Psalms 2:8 *"Ask of me, and I shall give thee the heathen for thine inheritance, and the uttermost parts of the earth for thy possession."* I declare that the prince of the air is bound from the souls of the lost. I loose the Anointing of God over all the lost, to remove the mind blocks. I declare the light of the glorious gospel of Christ, the image of God shining unto them, and I ask for their salvation. Please name the ones that you desire to be saved now; we agree on their salvation, in Jesus' name.

As in **II Corinthians 10:4,5,** I loose upon me, mighty weapons of warfare through God to the pulling down of strong holds: *"Casting down imaginations, and every high thing that exalteth itself against the knowledge of God, and bringing into captivity every thought to the obedience of Christ:" And,* in John **14:2** *" The comforter, which is the Holy Ghost, whom the Father will send in my name, He shall teach you all things, and bring all things to your remembrance, whatsoever I have said unto you."* I declare that I have a teachable spirit, supernatural wisdom, revelation knowledge, and supernatural learning abilities. I have a photographic memory, strong character, and open doors to success in all things. I loose the ability of God to declare the Word in faith, to co-create with God whatsoever I desire, in Jesus' name. I loose your Anointing God, to impart unto me the manifestation of the gifts of the Spirit, the word of wisdom, the word of knowledge, faith, the gifts of healing, the working of miracles, prophecy, discernment of spirits, tongues and interpretations, dividing unto me severally as you will, that I may profit with all. I declare, that all the gifts of the Spirit are operating in my life, and my footsteps are guided and directed by Almighty God. I am a soul winner, bold for Christ, faithful and steadfast in the Lord, and I use my talents and gifts to glorify you, Lord. I receive what I ask for, and find what I'm looking for.

I plead the blood of Jesus and loose the anointing of the healing virtue of Jesus Christ over me from top to bottom, throughout every system of my body, for the perfect functioning of each of my body systems, for total healing. I declare that I am strong, happy, and walk in divine health all the days of my long life.

I am the head and not the tail, above only, and not beneath, and I can do all things through Christ who strengthens me, and who always gives me peace, security, the favor of God and man, riches and honor. Victory in all things is mine, my whole life through. I will always triumph over all opposition, because it is my heritage as a child of the living God. I decree that our home is as the days of heaven on earth, **Deuteronomy 11:18-21.**

I declare that I have the power, the ability, and the Anointing of God to get wealth to establish God's covenant. I loose the anointing of God over me for restoration of life and nourishment.

I claim the laws of restitution to be operational in my life, that God may retrieve, reverse and return to the maximum all that I've lost. I pray for a window of Prophetic revelation to open, plans for my success, and prosperity in all things to unfold. God is my source, I am a covenant partner with God, and I am blessed. I declare and decree, that signs and wonders, many miracles, and supernatural signs of prosperity in all things, will follow me all the days of my long life. I am in alignment with God's Word.

I live under an open heaven, and I always walk in excess, in overflow, in the divine provision of God, the director of my path.

The extreme favor of God and man is over my life, and I will fulfill the calling and destiny that God has planned for me. I loose God's Anointing upon me, for Supernatural power to get wealth: empowerment through dreams, visions, ideas, wisdom and inventions. I declare an exponential multiplication of all my good seed sown, and total crop failure of any bad seed sown. I declare and claim, I plead the blood of Jesus and loose the Anointing of God for supernatural miracle power, for the provision of all my needs and desires, and for every covenant promise for prosperity, in all things.

I loose the Anointing of God for all positive ancestral, generational inheritances and blessings to ascend upon me. I decree that God is increasing my territory, and I am victorious and triumphant in all things through Christ Jesus! **Job 22:28** *"Thou shalt also decree a thing, and it shall be established unto thee:"* I have given voice to my covenant, your Word Father, and I loose the power and the Anointing of God to bind unto me all of these wonderful blessings, all of my covenant promises. I thank you, Father, that you watch over your Word to perform it. My guardian, bidding, ministering angels, and the angels of the Lord, are now loosed to establish this earnest petition, these declarations and decrees; and to bring all this good to me, for your glory, Lord. I bind them unto me, and give thanks unto God in the name of our Lord Jesus Christ. *" Be it unto me according to thy Word,"* as Mary said to the angel, in **Luke 1:38.** It is established, in Jesus' name. Amen!

<u>NOTES</u>

Daily Prayer - Five Minute

I put on the whole armor of God that I may be able to stand against the wiles of the devil. I put on the breastplate of righteousness, the helmet of salvation; my loins are gird about with truth, my feet shod with the preparation of the gospel of peace. I take the shield of faith to quench the fiery darts of the wicked, and the sword of the Spirit, the Word of God, to defeat Satan on every hand.

I apply the blood of Jesus to me, from the top of my head to the soles of my feet, for protection from all evil. I ask, Lord, that this same armor and blood protection, be placed on and around my spouse, children, pastors, family members; and everything I pray for myself, I pray for each of them, in Jesus' name.

I address, rebuke, and bind you Satan, every fallen angel and demon from the pit of hell, all evil principalities, powers, rulers of the darkness of this world, spiritual wickedness in high places, the prince of the air, kings, peoples, nobles, nations, and every evil spirit and power that you rule, command and have jurisdiction over, and I cast everyone of you into outer darkness, in Jesus' name.

I bind all demonic assignments against us, and cast them into the sea, and, I rebuke, and reverse all curses against us, and our households, in Jesus' name Amen.

1. **Our Dear Heavenly Father,** I come into your gates with thanksgiving and into your courts with praise, by the blood of Jesus.
2. I seek first the Kingdom of God and His Righteousness.
3. I declare I serve the King of Kings, and the Lord of Lords.
4. I worship and praise you, Father. You are my Redeemer, my Shepherd, my Strong Tower, and my Deliverer.
5. I declare that all the gifts of the Spirit are operational in my life.
6. I declare my faith fails not, and I pass every test.
7. I rejoice because of heaven, and that my name is written in the Lamb's Book of Life.
8. I repent and ask forgiveness of anything I've done, said or thought, unpleasing in your sight, Lord.
9. I declare God's protection and deliverance from all evil.
10. I loose God's Anointing over me for travel protection, travel mercies, and grace. I declare that no weapon formed against me shall prosper, and everything I do shall prosper. Every obstacle shall fall and every crooked place will be made straight.
11. No evil shall befall me; neither shall any plague come near my dwelling.
12. God's angels have charge over me, to keep me in all my ways. They bear me up in their hands, lest I dash my foot against a stone. I loose the anointing and the protection of God over our president, military, and our citizens in every country. I pray for America, Jerusalem, Israel, and I ask for God's Kingdom to be realized on earth as it is in heaven.
13. I ask for laborers to be sent into your harvest, Lord, and for salvation of all lost souls.
14. I loose God's anointing over all Christian ministers and saints, and declare that we are all equipped with the five-fold ministry operating in us.
15. I am an ambassador for Christ, a soul winner, and God orders my steps. I loose and receive the Anointing of God for the mind of Christ, His Supernatural wisdom, His learning abilities and His revelation knowledge.
16. I loose and receive the Anointing of God for a photographic memory with instant recall, strong character, integrity, and

open doors to all success.

17. I am the head and not the tail, above only, and not beneath;
18. I declare God's Word in faith, to co-create with God whatsoever I desire.
19. I am bold for Christ, faithful and steadfast in the Lord.
20. I loose the Anointing of the healing power of Jesus Christ over me, throughout every system of my body, for the perfect functioning of each; for total healing.
21. I am strong, happy, and walk in divine health all the days of my long life.
22. I can do all things through Christ who strengthens me, and who gives me peace, joy, security, riches, honor, and the extreme favor of God, and man.
23. Victory in all things, in every situation and circumstance is mine my whole life through. I always triumph over all opposition; and declare, that my home is as the days of heaven on earth.
24. I loose the power, ability, and the Anointing of God to get wealth, to establish God's covenant. I loose and receive all of the benefits, and covenant blessings that God's Word promises me.
25. I live under an open heaven, I am blessed to be a blessing, and I will fulfill the calling and destiny of God over my life.
26. The law of restitution is operational in my life, and God is retrieving, reversing and returning to the maximum, all that I've lost.
27. I decree, loose and receive signs and wonders, many miracles, and supernatural signs of prosperity in all things to follow me all the days of my long life.
28. I loose all positive ancestral, generational inheritances and blessings upon me.
29. God is increasing my territory, and I am victorious, and triumphant in all things.

I receive and bind all these covenant promises to me, and loose all the angels needed to establish these declarations and decrees. I ask the Lord to perform my words that I have prophesied.

"**Be it unto me according to thy Word,**" In Jesus' name, Amen.

PART IV. God's Greatest Gifts

Chapter Seven
Salvation

If you have read this far and have not given your heart to the Lord Jesus Christ, you must be searching for more; Something to fill your heart and your life with the forgiveness and the love of a mighty, awesome, wonderful God, and Saviour: A force in which you will have power; power over all the forces of evil, that come against you. **In Ezekiel 18:21, 22** we are told, *"But if the wicked will turn from all his sins that he hath committed, and keep all my statutes, and do that which is lawful and right, he shall surely live, he shall not die. All his transgressions that he hath committed, they shall not be mentioned unto him: in his righteousness that he hath done he shall live."* And in *Matthew 9:13* we are told, *"...for I am not come to call the righteous, but sinners to repentance."* **Mark 1:15** *"...The time is fulfilled, and the Kingdom of God is at hand: repent ye, and believe the gospel."* **Job.11:14, 15,** *"If iniquity be in thine hand, put it far away, and let not wickedness dwell in thy tabernacles. For then shalt thou lift up thy face without spot; yea, thou shalt be steadfast, and shalt not fear:"* **Psalms 147:3,** *"He healeth the broken in heart, and bindeth up their wounds."* And, praise God, we are told in **Psalms 34:18**, that, *"The Lord is nigh unto them that are of a broken heart; and saveth such as be of a contrite spirit."*

John 3:3-7, *"Jesus answered and said unto him, Verily, verily, I say unto thee, Except a man be born again, he cannot see the Kingdom of God. Nicodemus saith unto him, How can a man be born when he is old? Can he enter the second time into his mother's womb, and be born? Jesus answered, Verily, verily, I say unto thee, Except a man be born of water and of the Spirit, he cannot enter into the Kingdom of God. That which is born of the flesh is flesh; and that which is born of the Spirit is Spirit. Marvel not that I said unto thee, Ye must be born again."*

John 3:16 *"For God so loved the world, that He gave His one and only begotten Son, that, whosoever believeth in Him should* not perish, but have everlasting life."

I John 4:9 *"In this was manifested the love of God toward us, because that God sent His only begotten Son into the world, that we might live through Him."*

John 10:9,10,11 *"I am the door: by me if any man enter in, he shall be saved, and shall go in and out, and find pasture. The thief cometh not, but for to steal, and to kill, and to destroy: I am come that they might have life, and that they might have it more abundantly. I am the good shepherd: the good shepherd giveth His life for the sheep."*

John 5:24 *"Verily, verily, I say unto you, He that heareth My Word, and believeth on him that sent me, hath everlasting life, and shall not come into condemnation; but is passed from death unto life."*

Acts 2:21 *"...whosoever shall call on the name of the Lord shall be saved."*

Jeremiah 29:11-14 *"For I know the thoughts that I think toward you, saith the Lord, thoughts of peace, and not of evil, to give you an expected end. Then shall ye call upon me, and I will hearken unto you. And ye shall seek me, and find me, when ye shall search for me with all your heart. And I will be found of you, saith the Lord."*

Acts 4:12 *"Neither is there salvation in any other: for there is none other name under heaven given among men, whereby we must be saved."*

Acts 3:19, *"Repent ye therefore, and be converted, that your sins may be blotted out, when the times of refreshing shall come from the presence of the Lord."*

II Corinthians 5: 21 *"For He hath made Him to be sin for us, who knew no sin; that we might be made the righteousness of God in Him."*

Romans 6:14,22,23 *"For sin shall not have dominion over you: for ye are not under the law, but under grace." "...But now being made free from sin, and become servants to God, ye have your fruit unto holiness, and the end everlasting life. For the wages of sin is death; but, the gift of God is eternal life through Jesus Christ our Lord."*

II Timothy 1:9,10 *"Who hath saved us, and called us with an holy calling, not according to our works, but according to His own* *purpose and grace, which was given us in Christ Jesus before the world began, But is now made manifest by the appearing of our Saviour Jesus Christ, who hath abolished death, and hath brought life and immortality to light through the gospel:"*

I John 4:15 "Whosoever shall confess that Jesus is the Son of God, God dwelleth in him, and he in God."

I John 1:9 *"If we confess our sins, He is faithful and just to forgive us our sins, and to cleanse us from all unrighteousness."*

Hebrews 8:12 *"For I will be merciful to their unrighteousness, and their sins and their iniquities will I remember no more."*

After we have given our hearts and our lives to God, we are told in **II Corinthians 5:17**, **"Therefore if any man be in Christ, he is a new creature: old things are passed away; behold, all things are become new."** We are also told in **John 1:12, 13, "But as many as received Him, to them gave He power to become the sons of God, even to them that believe on His name: Which were born, not of blood, nor of the will of the flesh, nor of the will of man, but of God."**

Galations 2:20 *"I am crucified with Christ: nevertheless I live; yet not I, but Christ liveth in me: and the life which I now live in the flesh I live by the faith of the Son of God, who loved me, and gave himself for me."*

Ephesians 2:4-9 *"But God, who is rich in mercy, for His great love wherewith He loved us, Even when we were dead in sins, hath quickened us together with Christ, (by grace ye are saved;) And hath raised us up together, and made us sit together in heavenly places in Christ Jesus. That in the ages to come He might shew the exceeding riches of His grace in His kindness toward us through Christ Jesus. For by grace are ye saved through faith; and that not of yourselves: it is the gift of God: Not of works, lest any man should boast."*

Psalms 20:5 *"We will rejoice in thy salvation, and in the name of our God we will set up our banners: the Lord fulfill all thy petitions."*

<u>NOTES</u>

Prayer Of Salvation

Paul tells us in **Romans 10:8-10** *"...The Word is nigh thee, even in thy mouth, and in thy heart: that is, the Word of faith, which we preach: That if thou shalt confess with thy mouth the Lord Jesus, and shalt believe in thine heart that God hath raised Him from the dead, thou shalt be saved. For with the heart man believeth unto righteousness; and with the mouth confession is made unto salvation."*

To receive salvation and forgiveness of your sins, pray the following prayer out loud:

Oh God, you said in the Bible, that whosoever shall call upon the name of the Lord, shall be saved. I call on you now. I ask you to save me. I ask you to forgive me. I repent of all my sins, and I surrender my life to you. I believe that Jesus Christ is the Son of God. I believe He died on the cross for our sins, and that He arose on the third day, for our victory. I believe that in my heart, and make confession with my mouth, that Jesus is my Lord, and my Savior. I receive eternal life! In Jesus' name, Amen.

Let me congratulate you for making the decision to give your heart to Jesus, and to be saved. I encourage you to find a faith filled church to go to, and to worship with other believers. I also encourage you to follow the commandment of Jesus on water baptism; then you are assured eternal life with Jesus Christ, our Lord.

One of Jesus' last instructions to His disciples before he ascended to heaven is in **Matthew 28:18-20**, *"And Jesus came and spake unto them, saying, All power is given unto me in heaven and in earth. Go ye therefore, and teach all nations, Baptizing them in the name of the Father, and of the Son, and of the Holy Ghost:*

Teaching them to observe all things whatsoever I have commanded you: and, lo, I am with you alway, even unto the end of the world. Amen." In **Acts 2:38, 39** we are given the name of the Father, the Son, and the Holy Ghost, where we are told: *"Then Peter said unto them, Repent, and be baptized every one of you in the name of Jesus Christ for the remission of* *sins, and ye shall receive the gift of the Holy Ghost. For the promise is unto you, and to your children, and to all that are afar off, even as many as the Lord our God shall call."*

Hebrews 7:24-27 *"But this man, because He continueth ever, hath an unchangeable priesthood. **Wherefore He is able also to save them to the uttermost that come unto God by Him, seeing He ever liveth to make intercession for them.** For such an high priest became us, who is holy, harmless, undefiled, separate from sinners, and made higher than the heavens; Who needeth not daily, as those high priests, to offer up sacrifice, first for His own sins, and then for the people's: for this He did once, when He offered up Himself."*

I Peter 1:3-4 *"Blessed be the God and Father of our Lord Jesus Christ, which according to His abundant mercy hath begotten us again unto a lively hope by the resurrection of Jesus Christ from the dead. To an inheritance incorruptible, and undefiled, and that fadeth not away, reserved in heaven for you."*

Hebrews 10:19-23 *"Having therefore, brethren, boldness to enter into the holiest by the Blood of Jesus, By a new and living way, which He hath consecrated for us, through the veil, that is to say, His flesh; And having an high priest over the house of God: Let us draw near with a true heart in full assurance of faith, having our hearts sprinkled from an evil conscience, and our bodies washed with pure water. <u>Let us hold fast the profession of our faith without wavering;(for he is faithful that promised).</u>"*

<u>Go to your Bible regularly, open it prayerfully, read it expectantly, pray and expect miracles!</u>

Chapter Eight
Deliverance Prayer
Reversing Curses and Scriptures

Dear Heavenly father, I boldly come before your throne of grace with my armor in place, and the blood of Jesus totally covering me, throughout every cell and fiber of my being.

I repent and ask your forgiveness, if I am now, or have ever, dominated or controlled anyone contrary to the perfect will of God. In the name of Jesus Christ, I now renounce, break and loose myself, and my children from all domination and subjection to our mothers, fathers, grandparents and any other human beings, living or dead who has ever in the past or is now dominating or controlling us in any way contrary to the perfect will of God.

In the name of Jesus, I renounce, break, bind and cast into the sea, away from me and my children, all psychic bondage, bonds of physical or mental illness and disease, and all curses upon me and my family lineage, as a result of sins, transgressions, iniquities, occult or psychic involvements of myself, my children, my parents, my ancestors, my spouse, parents of my spouse, their ancestors and all ex-spouses, their parents and their ancestors. Thank you Lord, for setting us Free!

In the name of Jesus, I rebuke, and bind away from me and my children, all evil spirits, curses, charms, vexes, hexes, spells, jinks, occult powers, psychic powers, witchcraft, sorcery and hypnotic influence that have been put on us or our family lineage, by any person, occult source or psychic source. I Command all connected, and related spirits to leave us, and be cast into outer darkness now, in Jesus' name!

I come to you, Lord, as my Deliverer, you know all of my problems, everything that binds, defiles and harasses me. I now refuse to accept anything from Satan. I now loose from my children and myself, every dark spirit, every satanic bondage, every spirit in us that is not the Spirit of God. I command all such spirits to leave us now, in Jesus' name. I declare that Satan has no place in us, and no power over us. In the name of Jesus Christ

I now break and reverse all curses against us according to Galations 3:13-14, and Colossians 2:13-15. I loose the Anointing of Jesus Christ over us for the total healing and protection of our souls, minds, bodies and spirits, in the name of Jesus. I confess that our bodies are temples of the Holy Ghost, redeemed, sanctified, cleansed, and justified by the Blood of Jesus Christ, and filled with the over coming power of the Lord.

Galations 3:13-14 *"Christ hath redeemed us from the curse of the law, being made a curse for us: for it is written, cursed is everyone that hangeth on a tree: That the blessing of Abraham might come on the gentiles through Jesus Christ; that we might receive the promise of the spirit through faith."*

Colossians 2:13-15 *"And you, being dead in your sins and the uncircumcision of your flesh, hath He quickened together with Him, having forgiven you all trespasses; Blotting out the hand writing of ordinances that was against us, which was contrary to us, and took it out of the way, nailing it to his cross. And having spoiled principalities and powers, He made a show of them openly, triumphing over them in it.* In I John 4:4 we are told, *"Ye are of God, little children, and have overcome them: because greater is He that is in you, than he that is in the world."*

Joel 2:32 *"And it shall come to pass, that whosoever shall call on the name of the Lord shall be delivered: for in mount Zion and in Jerusalem shall be deliverance, as the Lord hath said, and in the remnant whom the Lord shall call."*

I loose the Anointing of the protection of God over my children and I.

I THANK YOU LORD FOR SETTING US FREE, IN JESUS' NAME, AMEN!

Colossians 2:10 *"And ye are complete in Him, which is the head of all principality and power:"*

I Peter 2:24 *"Who his own self bare our sins in His own body on the tree, that we, being dead to sins, should live unto righteousness: by whose stripes ye were healed."*

Numbers 14:18 *" The Lord is longsuffering, and of great mercy, forgiving iniquity and transgression, and by no means clearing the guilty, visiting the iniquity of the fathers upon the* *children, unto the third and fourth generation.*"

Exodus 34:7 *"Keeping mercy for thousands, forgiving iniquity and transgression and sin, and that will by no means clear the guilty; visiting the iniquity of the fathers upon the children, and upon the children's children, unto the third and to the fourth generation."*

Deuteronomy 7:25,26, *"The graven images of their gods shall ye burn with fire: thou shalt not desire the silver or gold that is on them, nor take it unto thee, lest thou be snared therein: for it is an abomination to the Lord thy God. Neither shalt thou bring an abomination into thine house, lest thou be a cursed thing like it: but thou shalt utterly detest it, and thou shalt utterly abhor it, for it is a cursed thing."*

Galations 5:16-25 *"This I say then, walk in the spirit, and ye shall not fulfill the lust of the flesh. For the flesh lusteth against the Spirit, and the Spirit against the flesh: and these are contrary the one to the other: so that ye cannot do the things that ye would. But if ye be led of the Spirit, ye are not under the law. Now the works of the flesh are manifest, which are these; Adultery, fornication, uncleanness, lasciviousness, Idolatry, witchcraft, hatred, variance, emulations, wrath, strife, seditions, heresies, Envyings, murders, drunkenness, revellings, and such like: of the which I tell you before, as I have also told you in time past, that they which do such things shall not inherit the Kingdom of God. But the fruit of the Spirit is love, joy, peace, longsuffering, gentleness, goodness, faith, meekness, temperance: against such there is no law. And they that are Christ's have crucified the flesh with the affections and lusts. If we live in the Spirit, let us also walk in the Spirit."*

ROMANS 8:2 *"FOR THE LAW OF THE SPIRIT OF LIFE IN CHRIST JESUS HATH MADE ME FREE FROM THE LAW OF SIN AND DEATH."*

Psalms 91:11,12 *"For He shall give His angels charge over thee, to keep thee in all thy ways. They shall bear thee up in their hands, lest thou dash thy foot against a stone."*

II Timothy 4:18 *"And the Lord shall deliver me from every evil work, and will preserve me unto His heavenly Kingdom."*

Exodus 33:19 *"And He said, I will make all My goodness pass before thee, and I will proclaim the name of the Lord before thee;*

and will be gracious to whom I will be gracious, and will shew mercy on whom I will shew mercy."

Psalms 41:11,12 *"By this I know that thou favourest me, because mine enemy doth not triumph over me. And as for me, thou upholdest me in mine integrity, and settest me before thy face for ever."*

Job 10:12 *"Thou hast granted me life and favour, and thy visitation hath preserved my spirit."*

There are wonderful protection scriptures to stand on following the Protection Prayer on page 175.

<u>NOTES</u>

Chapter Nine

The Holy Ghost

The most fundamental, most key, element of being able to pray effectively is to be obedient to what God has put in place. We are His children, and He has given us His most precious, priceless gift, the gift of the Holy Ghost! God started the church in
Acts 2:38,39. *"Then Peter said unto them, repent, and be baptized every one of you in the name of Jesus Christ for the remission of sins, and ye shall receive the gift of the Holy Ghost. For the promise is unto you and to your children, and to all that are afar off, even as many as the Lord our God shall call."*

After Jesus ascended into heaven, people from all over the world heard the Galileans speak in unknown tongues. When you receive the Holy Ghost, your personal prayer language is given unto you; it flows out of you like a river. When you speak in tongues, you are speaking directly to God; speaking mysteries, hidden wisdom, divine secrets. The devil has no understanding of your heavenly language because God has hidden the meaning from him. God is praying through you when you pray in tongues, therefore your prayer is perfect.

Jude 1:20, *"But ye, beloved, building up yourselves on your most holy faith, praying in the Holy Ghost."* And,
I Corinthians 14:14 says, *"For if I pray in an unknown tongue, my spirit prayeth, but my understanding is unfruitful."* This is true communion with God; Unknown tongues come out of your spirit and you are praying secrets that only God knows. God is using your mouth to build you up, and to bring forth all these wonderful things. Your understanding doesn't know, only God knows.

The devil doesn't know those divine secrets either. God is a spirit, and your spirit is communing and connecting with God.
Romans 8:26-28, *"Likewise the Spirit also helpeth our infirmities: for we know not what we should pray for as we ought: but the Spirit itself maketh intercession for us with groanings which cannot be*

uttered. And He that searcheth the hearts knoweth what is the mind of the Spirit, because He maketh intercession for the saints according to the will of God. And we know that all things work together for good to them that love God, to them who are the called according to His purpose." You are praying out God's will when you pray in the Holy Ghost. There are many benefits to praying in the Holy Ghost.

To receive the Holy Ghost, you have to let your tongue be loose and God will give the utterance. This is both a natural, and a Supernatural experience. **"For *the Holy Ghost shall teach you in the same hour what ye ought to say,"* Luke 12:12.** And in **Luke 11:13, *"If ye then, being evil, know how to give good gifts unto your children: how much more shall your heavenly Father give the Holy Spirit to them that ask Him?"*** And **Romans 5:5** tells us that, *"...the love of God is shed abroad in our hearts by the Holy Ghost which is given unto us."*

I loose the Anointing of God to release the Holy Ghost, to set upon each person who has repented and who desires to receive the Holy Ghost; to set upon them like the fire of Pentecost, in **Acts 2:2- 4** *"And suddenly there came a sound from heaven as of a rushing mighty wind, and it filled all the house where they were sitting. And there appeared unto them cloven tongues like as of fire, and it sat upon each of them. And they were all filled with the Holy Ghost, and began to speak with other tongues, as the Spirit gave them utterance."*

In **Acts 1:4,5,8,** we are told, that (Jesus), *"...being assembled together with them, commanded them that they should not depart from Jerusalem, but wait for the promise of the Father, which, saith He, ye have heard of me. For John truly baptized with water; but ye shall be baptized with the Holy Ghost not many days hence. But ye shall receive power after that the Holy Ghost is come upon you: and ye shall be witnesses unto me..."*

Ask, and receive of the Father...and continue praying in tongues until relief comes, until you feel the peace of God, until you feel Victory!

If you have repented of all of your sins, and, If you desire the Holy Ghost, pray this now:

I loose the Anointing of God over me, to receive the outpouring of the Holy Ghost with the evidence of speaking in tongues. I receive with a hungry heart, the mighty, awesome, incomparable gift of God into my heart; To build up myself in faith, to pray secrets that only God knows, to help any, and all infirmities the enemy has, or may try to put on me, and to pray God's will. I thank you, heavenly Father, my omnipotent God Almighty, for this priceless gift, in Jesus' Name, Amen.

Acts 11:16 "…John indeed baptized with water; but ye shall be baptized with the Holy Ghost."

John 14:26 "But the comforter, which is the Holy Ghost, whom the Father will send in my name, He shall teach you all things, and bring all things to your remembrance, whatsoever I have said unto you."

Luke 11:13 "…how much more shall your heavenly Father give the Holy Spirit to them that ask Him?"

Luke 3:16 "John answered, saying unto them all, I indeed baptize you with water; but one mightier than I cometh, the latchet of whose shoes I am not worthy to unloose; He shall baptize you with the Holy Ghost and with fire:"

You can read more about the Holy Ghost throughout Acts, such as **in Acts 1:8, Acts 10:44, Acts 19:6,** and many other scriptures throughout the New Testament, after the Holy Ghost fell on the church on the day of Pentecost in **Acts 2:1- 4.**

PART V. Healing Revelations

Chapter Ten
Healing
Introduction

I come, in the name of Jesus, to bring God's Word for explanation and practical application concerning healing. Our heavenly Father has given us the authority to bind and to loose. The Word says, whatsoever we bind on earth will be bound in heaven, and whatsoever we loose on earth will be loosed in heaven. We are going to bind Satan and all evil, then, we will loose the healing virtue of Jesus Christ over you. As you pray along with me, we will confess and profess that which God says about you; we will declare your healing and God's Covenant promises over your life.

It is my desire to instill in you how to declare God's Word, and then to stand on God's Word, until you are totally recovered from any, and all sickness and disease. God's Word Works! It never fails. God's Word is omnipotent. It has unlimited authority, because God has unlimited authority; It is all-powerful. We see in **John 1:1,3,4** *"In the beginning was the Word, and the Word was with God, and the Word was God." "All things were made by Him; and without Him was not anything made that was made: In Him was life; and the life was the light of men."* <u>Isn't our God good? He has even put His life into us</u>. In **Romans 8:2** we are told, *"For the law of the Spirit of life in Christ Jesus hath made me free from the law of sin and death."*

Our God is omnipresent; He is in all places at the same time. Since the Word is God, then His Word is everywhere at all times also. When we honor and obey God by speaking His Word, He causes what we say to come to pass, because He watches over His Word, to perform it. Let's work with God, within the laws that He has established, to bring forth your healing.

In **Deuteronomy 8:3**, "*.... man doth not live by bread only, but by every Word that proceedeth out of the mouth of the Lord doth man live!*" And in **Hebrews 4:12** we're told, *"For the Word of God is quick,* [alive] *and powerful, and sharper than* *any two-edged sword, piercing even to the dividing asunder of soul and spirit, and of the joints and marrow, and is a discerner of the thoughts and intents of the heart."* <u>The Word of God is Alive, and it is powerful</u>!

We are coming together to confess and to profess God's Word over your life, and your situation. The Greek translation for confession means, "saying the same thing," and professes means to" declare one's belief in, to declare openly". **Hebrews 10:23 , "Let us hold fast the profession of our faith without wavering;(for He is faithful that promised.)"** When we say God's Word over our bodies or our situation in faith, believing, we give God something to work with, His Word! God is obligated to heal our bodies when we live for Him, and keep His commandments, because God is obligated to His Word! God watches over His Word to perform it.

Matthew 11:7-10, tells us that John the Baptist's ministry was to prepare the way of the Lord; to prepare the way for Jesus to come. His words were prophecy, He spoke! He prepared, He prophesied the way for Jesus. It is the same today; Jesus is obligated to come into the situation that we prophesy about. <u>We have Power! The power of life and death, is in our tongues. Let's speak the Word, Let's speak God's Words! When we speak God's Words, we are speaking life. We are coming to speak and to declare life and healing over your body, over your situation</u>.

When the prophets prophesied, they prophesied by the inspiration of God. <u>We are operating in the spirit of prophecy when we say, when we confess, and when we profess the Word</u>. **Jeremiah 1:12 "Then said the Lord unto me, thou hast well seen: for I will hasten** [which means to, hurry, accelerate, quicken, expedite] *my Word to perform it."* Hallelujah!

<u>We are coming together to prophesy your healing</u>. God used prophesying to bring all scriptures to fulfillment. We are backing up our words with the inspired Word of God. In the first chapter of **Genesis,** God used His Words to build and to frame His world. We likewise are to speak God's Words over our world, to frame our world, like God did. <u>Your mouth, what you</u> <u>speak, your word, prophesies your future</u>. God's Word works! Let's work God's Words! Let us work God's Words to make some changes. Let us change some things! Let us change your health situation; let us bring life, God's life into your situation. Let us say what God Said!

Let us believe God! God's Word is forever true, it never changes, it never fails, and it most assuredly changes things! **Ephesians 3:20,** *"Now unto Him that is able to do exceeding abundantly above all that we ask or think, according to the power that worketh in us."* Isn't it wonderful that our God can do more than we can even think, or ask? By the Holy Ghost, His power that is at work in us.

The spoken Word of God is creative power, it was creative power when God spoke it, and it is creative power today, when we speak it. What we speak, the words which come out of our mouths, are words of prophecy, and they create our future. In **Genesis 1:27** we are told, *"So God created man in His own image,"* and in **Mark 11:22-24** Jesus told us, whosoever shall say, have faith, believe, and doubt not, can have whatsoever they say. Things that we say, shall come to pass. Let's say what God said! When we speak God's Words, God is obligated to bring them to pass; God Keeps His Word.

The scripture also tells us that God's Word is above all of His name! God's Word stands forever. It is eternal. When we pray, we are giving God permission to intervene for us on this earth. When we speak God's faith filled Words, mix our faith with God's faith filled Words, they bring God's action into this world and they create things. **Hebrews 11:3** *"Through faith we understand that the worlds were framed by the Word of God, so that things which are seen were not made of things which do appear."* Hebrews **11:1** tells us that, *"Now faith is the substance of things hoped for."* God also responds to persistence. **Hebrews 11:6,** *"...for he that cometh to God must believe that He is, and that He is a rewarder of them that diligently seek Him."* When we seek God diligently, believing, praying in faith, we are assured that He will reward us. Our faith is rewarded by our diligence, perseverance, and persistence. The definition of persevere in Webster's New Complete Thesaurus, is to "continue in a state, enterprise or undertaking in spite of counter influence, or opposition, or discouragement; to carry on, go on, hang on, persist, to continue, press on, proceed." And if we proceed, we advance, we move on, we continue. The definition of persistent in the same Thesaurus is, "continuing in a course of action without regard to discouragement, opposition, or previous failure. To be insistent, persevering, persisting, determined, steadfast, tenacious, unshakable, relentless, unremitting, without yielding, vacillating, or wavering."

Paul says in **I Timothy 2:8,** *"I will therefore that men pray everywhere, lifting up holy hands, without wrath and doubting."* We must believe, believe God, and believe God's Word. God said that He has given every man a measure of faith. If you desire then, to have great faith, it is up to you to grow more faith. Faith cometh by hearing, and hearing by the Word of God. To grow more faith, you must speak the Word, hear the Word, believe the Word and live the Word! Faith guarantees the results of prayer as we are told in **Mark 11:22-24.** *"…Have faith in God. For verily I say unto you, That whosoever shall say unto this mountain, Be thou removed, and be thou cast into the sea; and shall not doubt in his heart, but shall believe that those things which he saith shall come to pass; he shall have whatsoever he saith. Therefore I say unto you, What things soever ye desire, when ye pray, believe that ye receive them, and ye shall have them."*

When you pray the Word, you are praying God's will, because God's will is His Word. **Luke 17:6** *"And the Lord said, If ye had faith as a grain of mustard seed, ye might say unto this sycamine tree, Be thou plucked up by the root, and be thou planted in the sea; and it should obey you."*

The apostles asked the Lord in **Luke 17:5,** *"…Lord, Increase our faith."* Therefore, we know that our faith is capable of increasing if we feed it God's Word.

Romans 10:8 *"…The Word is nigh thee, even in thy mouth, and in thy heart;"* As you pray along with me, believe God. Believe His Words and have great desire. As we prophesy, as we speak all of these wonderful blessings and covenant promises over our lives, we need to desire, to yearn strongly for that for which we pray. Keep God's Words in your minds and in your hearts. Meditate on God's Word. We are told in **Matthew 11:12,** *"And from the days of John the Baptist until now the kingdom of heaven suffereth violence, and the violent take it by force."* Believe, doubt not, desire! Be persistent with your prayers, continuing to pray them daily, or better yet- several times a day. We have a mandate from God Almighty to pray. Refuse to quit, until you receive, that for which you ask. **Matthew 7:7** *"Ask, and it shall be given you; seek, and ye shall find; knock, and it shall be* *opened unto you:"* Jesus told His disciples in **Luke 18:1, "...** *that men ought always to pray..."* (Which indicates continuing, more than once, ongoing if you will), and not to faint!

We know that the persistent widow in the parable given by Jesus in **Luke 18:2-8,** received what she repeatedly asked for from the judge because he did not want to be bothered with her coming continually, asking for the same thing. The judge said in **v.5,** *"...I will avenge her, lest by her continual coming she weary me."* And we are told in **James 5:16** that it is, "The *effectual fervent prayer of a righteous man* (that) *availeth much."*

Jacob, who wrestled with an angel all night and told him, that he would not let him go until he blessed him, shows perseverance in prayer. Jacob received his blessing. Daniel prayed 21 days, before his answer came. Daniel's answer was delayed, blocked, by the prince of Persia, until Michael, the Archangel of God, intervened. The Syrophenician woman repeatedly brought her request to the Lord to heal her daughter, while Jesus ignored her cry. She continued pursuing after Him, worshiping Him, and crying, "Lord, Help me!" He did. **Matthew 15:28** tells us, that the Lord healed her daughter that very hour. This mother would not give up. She persisted continually until she received of the Lord. Her faith, desire, and persistence, conquered all of her obstacles. Let us therefore be diligent, and fervent. Let us continually confess God's Word, our covenant rights, our blessings, our healing, until we receive from the Lord, that which we declare.

Jesus also admonishes us in **Luke 21:36,** to, *"Watch ye therefore, and pray always, that ye may be accounted worthy to escape all these things that shall come to pass, and to stand before the Son of man."*

If you have not yet put on the armor of God, applied the blood of Jesus over you, and bound Satan and all evil from you today, go to page 106 and do so now. Then we will profess, confess God's Words, and loose God's blessings, His covenant promises of healing over you. The enemy comes to kill, to steal and to destroy. God came that we might have life, and have it more abundantly! Let's profess His Word! Are you ready?

Follow after me.

A Healing Decree

This decree and declaration claims and professes total healing, wholeness, prosperity, complete restoration of my mind, body, soul, and spirit, according to God's Kingdom laws, in Jesus' name; Shalom, With nothing missing, nothing broken!

I bind Satan, every demonic spirit, including the spirit of infirmities, and the prince of the air, away from me, and my health, and cast them all into outer darkness, in Jesus' name.

Matthew 16:19 tells us, *"And I will give unto thee the keys of the kingdom of heaven: and whatsoever thou shalt bind on earth shall be bound in heaven: and whatsoever thou shalt loose on earth shall be loosed in heaven."*

I bind, command, and say to every assignment of evil against my body, be thou removed, and be thou cast into the sea. All assignments of sickness, disease, viruses, allergies, unfriendly bacteria, weakness, pain, and any problem that tries to attach itself to me in any part of my body, be thou removed, and be thou cast into the sea, in Jesus' name. All sickness, disease, and symptoms are illegal in my body, and have to go. They have no right and no authority in me. My body is the temple of the Lord. Under the protection of the Blood of Jesus Christ, and with the authority vested in me by Christ Himself, I declare that I am redeemed from the curse of the law, by the Blood of the Lamb.

Colossians 2:13-15 *"And you, being dead in your sins and the uncircumcision of your flesh, hath he quickened together with Him, having forgiven you all trespasses: Blotting out the handwriting of ordinances that was against us, which was contrary to us, and took it out of the way, nailing it to His cross: And having spoiled principalities and powers, He made a shew of them openly, triumphing over them in it."*

I am delivered from all disease, sickness and pain, because I receive the Spirit through faith. I overcome you Satan by the blood of the Lamb, and by the word of my testimony, **Revelation 12:11.** In **Romans 8:2** we're told, *"For the Law of the Spirit of life in Christ Jesus hath made me free from the law of sin and death."* God's Word is eternal truth! I stand on God's laws, the written Word of God, in Jesus' name, Amen. Sign below and date.

HEALING PRAYER

Our dear Heavenly Father, I come to you by the authority given me by Jesus Christ, our mediator and Chief High Priest, to declare total, complete healing, with full restoration of my mind, body, soul, and spirit. I am redeemed from the curse of the law, by the blood of the Lamb, because of **Galations 3:13.** *Christ was made a curse for us,* **"Christ hath redeemed us from the curse of the law, being made a curse for us, for it is written, cursed is every one that hangeth on a tree: That the blessing of Abraham might come on the Gentiles through Jesus Christ; that we might receive the promise of the Spirit through faith."**

I claim the power and benefit of **Psalms 118:17,** **"I shall not die, but live, and declare the works of the Lord."** We are told in **Leviticus 17:11,** that the life of the flesh is in the blood; so I claim that your abundant life, Jesus, is present in my blood and my entire body now. **Genesis 4:10,** and **I John 5:8,** declares the blood is a witness, and **Hebrews 12:24** tells us, the blood speaks. So I ask the precious blood of Jesus, to speak continually on my behalf, for complete healing, and total restoration.

Joel 3:21 **"For I will cleanse their blood that I have not cleansed: for the Lord dwelleth in Zion."** I thank you, Father, that you are cleansing my blood, every minute of every hour, day and night. I declare that my blood is kept clean by your cleansing power! I receive the Spirit through faith. God's Word is eternally true! I declare Victory over all sickness, and disease in my mind, and in my body, because **Mark 11:24** says, I shall have what I say, if I do not doubt; and, that I shall reap if I faint not.

I declare that my immune system is strong, healthy, alert, and kills every foreign invader of all kinds. My body only produces cells with perfect RNA, and perfect DNA. Every cell in my body has a protective shield of God's mercy, grace, strength, and divine health, surrounding it. My spirit is filled with the overcoming joy of the Lord. I thank you, God, that when I pray the Word, I am praying the will of God.

Jeremiah 1:12 says, **"...I will hasten** (be alert and active over) **My Word to perform it:"** I John 3:22, **"And whatsoever we ask, we receive of Him, because we keep His commandments, and**

do those things that are pleasing in His sight." I believe I receive when I ask.

I John 5:14,15 *"And this is the confidence that we have in Him, that, if we ask any thing according to His will, He heareth us: And if we know that He hear us, whatsoever we ask, we know that we have the petitions that we desired of Him."*

I loose the power of all these healing scriptures that I am standing on, into my mind and into my body. I loose the Anointing of the healing virtue of Jesus Christ throughout my body for total, complete healing, from the crown of my head to the soles of my feet. I declare total restoration, In Jesus' name.

I thank you, God, that the yoke is destroyed because of the Anointing, according to **Isaiah 10:27. We're told in Psalms 103:2- 5,** to *"Bless the Lord, Oh my soul, and forget not all his benefits: Who forgiveth all thine iniquities; who healeth all thine diseases; Who redeemeth thy life from destruction; who crowneth thee with loving kindness and tender mercies; Who satisfieth thy mouth with good things; so that thy youth is renewed like the eagle's."*

Romans 8:11 *"But if the Spirit of Him that raised up Jesus from the dead dwell in you, He that raised up Christ from the dead shall also quicken your mortal bodies by His Spirit that dwelleth in you."*

Acts 27:25, *"Wherefore, sirs...I believe God, that it shall be even as it was told me."* I believe the report of the Lord, and I claim victory, wholeness, and restoration of my body, mind, soul, and spirit, as you've promised in your Word.

I am putting you in remembrance, Lord, and I am standing, as we are told in **Ephesians 6:14**, until victory is manifested for me. I declare that I will die in my full strength, being wholly at ease, and quiet, completely secure, my body well nourished; and my bones rich with marrow, as in **Job 21:23, 24,** after living in divine health, all the days of my long life.

I confess and declare all of God's promises to me are "Yes", and "Amen". I thank you, Father, that your Anointing is activated in my body right now, and your quickening Spirit is fully restoring me to complete health. I am reminding you, Lord, of your covenant promises of healing by bringing your Word before you, and by standing on your Word! I thank you for **Luke 1:37, 38** which tells me, *"For with God nothing shall be impossible," "…. be it unto me according to thy Word."* I give you thanks, and praise, Father, in Jesus' name. *Amen and Amen!*

NOTES

Faith And Healing Scriptures

Now that you have prayed and declared your healing, and before praying the following healing scriptures, I want to share a story with you, because the devil (your enemy), does not want you to receive your healing. Remember, he has come to kill, to steal, and to destroy.

There are different ways in which the Lord heals; one way is by divine healing, where one is healed immediately and completely. Another way is the way that most people are healed- by recovery!

I was fortunate to have been raised by loving parents in a wonderful, Spirit filled church in central Louisiana. As a child growing up, if anything was wrong with me (such as colds, or flu), I went forward at church for prayer, again and again, until I was well. I wondered why God didn't heal me immediately the first time. After all, my pastor prayed a great anointed prayer and anointed me with oil, as in **James 5:14,15.** I thought I had to keep getting the pastor to pray until I received my immediate healing. I didn't realize that God has given us, as individuals, the greatest part of the responsibility for receiving our healing.

In **Mark 11:22-24,** Jesus tells us to, *"…Have faith in God. For verily I say unto you, That whosoever shall say unto this mountain, be thou removed, and be thou cast into the sea; and shall not doubt in his heart, but shall believe that those things which he saith shall come to pass; he shall have whatsoever he saith."* We have things to do; we have to cast our mountain of (sickness or whatever), into the sea. We have to believe, we have to say, doubting not. And then we can have whatsoever we say, as long as we live for God, and keep His commandments. God expects us to take part in our healing.

Jeff Hackleman, the senior pastor at Family Faith Church in Huntsville, Texas, is an awesome pastor, from whom I have learned so very much. He has the amazing, anointed, ability to put things on a level that can be understood by everyone. The following is my version of his wonderful story of healing by recovery.

Pastor Jeff said, "I went to the hospital to see my good friend Bob, who recently had surgery. I was shocked to find Bob out of it.

He didn't even know I was there. He had wires and tubes running out of him everywhere; he was hooked up to all kinds of machines. I knew he was sick, but I wasn't prepared for what I found. He really, really looked bad. I walked out into the hall to see if I could find anyone that could tell me what had happened to my friend Bob, because he looked so awful. Coming up the hall was Bob's doctor. I asked him if he could tell me how my friend Bob was doing? The doctor beamed, he smiled from ear to ear, and said, "Oh, Bob is doing great! He has had a successful surgery, and <u>he is just recovering</u>."

It is the same way when we pray, decree, and confess the Word for our healing. We are just recovering. When the enemy brings an assignment of pain, nausea, or anything that would harm or hurt us, we know that it is a lying assignment from the devil. The Word tells us to rebuke the devil, and he will flee. Rebuke all symptoms in the name of Jesus, and they have to flee.

While you are recovering, let me caution you to "BE IN CONTROL OF YOUR EMOTIONS!" Do not be angry, do not be frustrated: Negative emotions will block the wonderful, healing power of the Lord. **James 1:19, 20, *"Wherefore, my beloved brethren, let every man be swift to hear, slow to speak, slow to wrath: For the wrath of man worketh not the righteousness of God."*** We are also told in **John 14:1, *"Let not your heart be troubled."*** <u>This indicates that we have a choice</u>. Don't let anyone, family, friends, or anything steal your joy, your faith, or your hope. Meditate on the Lord and good things only. **Romans 15:13, *"Now the God of hope fill you with all joy and peace in believing, that ye may abound in hope, through the power of the Holy Ghost."*** Keep yourself firmly planted in the Kingdom of God.

Romans 14:17, *"For the Kingdom of God is not meat and drink; but righteousness, and peace, and joy in the Holy Ghost."* <u>Keep the Holy Ghost stirred within you, stay in peace and joy</u>. **Romans 14;19, *"Let us therefore follow after the things which make for peace, and things wherewith one may edify another."*** And in **II Timothy 1:7, *"For God hath not given us the spirit of fear; but of power, and of love, and of a sound mind."*** **Luke 6:45, *"A good man out of the good treasure of his heart bringeth forth that which is good; and an evil man out of the***

evil treasure of his heart bringeth forth that which is evil; for of the abundance of the heart his mouth speaketh." Keep therefore your heart overflowing with the love, peace and joy of the Lord, so your mouth speaks and professes that which you desire to bring forth, in this case, your healing!

Psalms 119:170, 172, *"Let my supplication come before thee: deliver me according to thy Word." "My tongue shall speak of thy Word: for all thy commandments are righteousness."* As Paul wrote in **I Thessalonians,** chapter **5,** verses **16-24,** *"Rejoice evermore. Pray without ceasing. In every thing give thanks: for this is the will of God in Christ Jesus concerning you. Quench not the Spirit. Despise not prophesyings. Prove all things; hold fast that which is good. Abstain from all appearance of evil. And the very God of peace sanctify you wholly; and I pray God your whole spirit and soul and body be preserved blameless unto the coming of our Lord Jesus Christ. Faithful is he that calleth you, who also will do it."*

Romans 8:2, *"For the law of the Spirit of life in Christ Jesus hath made me free from the law of sin and death."*

Romans 8:11, *"But if the Spirit of Him that raised up Jesus from the dead dwell in you, He that raised up Christ from the dead shall also quicken your mortal body by His Spirit that dwelleth in you."*

Psalms 118:1, *"I shall not die, but live, and declare the works of the Lord."*

Proverbs 4:20-22, *"My son, attend to my Words; incline thine ear unto my sayings. Let them not depart from thine eyes; keep them in the midst of thine heart. For they are life unto those that find them, and health to all their flesh."*

Isaiah 53:4, 5, *"Surely He hath borne our griefs, and carried our sorrows: yet we did esteem Him stricken, smitten of God, and afflicted. But He was wounded for our transgressions, He was bruised for our iniquities: the chastisement of our peace was upon Him; and with His stripes we are healed."*

I Peter 2:24, *"Who His own self bare our sins in His own body on the tree, that we, being dead to sins, should live unto righteousness: by whose stripes ye were healed."*

Proverbs 3:1,2, *"My son, forget not my law; but let thine* *heart keep My commandments; For length of days, and long life, and peace, shall they add to thee."*

Deuteronomy 5:33, *"Ye shall walk in all the ways which the Lord your God hath commanded you, that ye may live, and that it may be well with you, and that ye may prolong your days in the land which ye shall possess."*

Proverbs 10:27, *"The fear of the Lord prolongeth days:"*

Proverbs 9:11, *"For by me thy days shall be multiplied, and the years of thy life shall be increased."*

Deuteronomy 6:2, *"That thou mightest fear the Lord thy God, to keep all His statutes and His commandments, which I command thee, thou, and thy son, and thy son's son, all the days of thy life; and that thy days may be prolonged."*

Matthew 9:28-30, *"And when He was come into the house, the blind men came to Him: And Jesus saith unto them, Believe ye that I am able to do this? They said unto Him, Yea, Lord. Then touched He their eyes, saying, according to your faith be it unto you. And their eyes were opened."*

Mark 9:23, "**Jesus said unto him, If thou can'st believe, all things are possible to him that believeth.**"

Jeremiah 17:14, *"Heal me, O Lord, and I shall be healed; save me, and I shall be saved: for thou art my praise."*

Matthew 4:23, 24, *"And Jesus went about all Galilee, teaching in their synagogues, and preaching the gospel of the Kingdom, and healing all manner of sickness and all manner of disease among the people. And His fame went throughout all Syria:* ***and they brought unto Him all sick people that were taken with divers diseases and torments, and those which were possessed with devils, and those which were lunatic, and those that had the palsy; and He healed them."***

Exodus 23:25, *"And ye shall serve the Lord your God, and He shall bless thy bread, and thy water; and I will take sickness away from the midst of thee."*

Psalms 31:23,24, *" O Love the Lord, all ye His saints: For the Lord preserveth the faithful, and plentifully rewardeth the proud doer. Be of good courage, and He shall strengthen your heart, all ye that hope in the Lord."*

Isaiah 35:4-6, *"Say to them that are of a fearful heart, Be* *strong, fear not: Behold, your God will come with vengeance, even God with a recompense; He will come and save you. Then the eyes of the blind shall be opened, and the ears of the deaf shall be unstopped. Then shall the lame man leap as an hart, and the tongue of the dumb sing."*

Psalms 147:3, *"He healeth the broken in heart, and bindeth up their wounds."*

Psalms 29:11, *"The Lord will give strength unto His people; The Lord will bless His people with peace."*

Isaiah 54:17, *"No weapon that is formed against thee shall prosper;"*

Psalms 27:14, *"Wait on the Lord: Be of good courage, and He shall strengthen thine heart: Wait, I say, on the Lord."*

Psalms 34:19,20, *"Many are the afflictions of the righteous: but the Lord delivereth him out of them all. He keepeth all his bones: not one of them is broken."*

Isaiah 26:4, *"Trust ye in the Lord forever; for in the Lord Jehovah is everlasting strength:"*

Matthew 9:22, To the woman with an issue of blood, Jesus said, **"Daughter, Be of good comfort; thy faith hath made thee whole."**

Matthew 11:5, **"The blind receive their sight, and the lame walk, the lepers are cleansed, and the deaf hear, the dead are raised up, and the poor have the gospel preached to them."**

Matthew 7:7,8, **"Ask, and it shall be given you; seek, and ye shall find; knock, and it shall be opened unto you: For every one that asketh receiveth; and he that seeketh findeth; and to him that knocketh it shall be opened."**

Isaiah 30:19, *" ..He will be very gracious unto thee at the voice of thy cry; when He shall hear it, He will answer thee."*

John 15:7, *" If ye abide in me, and My Words abide in you, ye shall ask what ye will, and it shall be done unto you."*

Philippians 4:7, **"And the peace of God, which passeth all understanding, shall keep your hearts and minds through Christ Jesus."**

Luke 7:50, **"**...*Thy faith hath saved thee; go in peace."*

John 14:27, **"Peace I leave with you, My peace I give unto you: not as the world giveth, give I unto you. Let not your Heart be troubled, neither let it be afraid**.*"*

Hebrews 10:23, *"Let us hold fast the profession of our faith without wavering; (For He is faithful that promised:)"*

Deuteronomy 30:15,16, *"See, I have set before thee this day life and good, and death and evil; In that I command thee this day to love the Lord thy God, to walk in His ways, and to keep His commandments and His statutes and His judgments, that thou mayest live and multiply: and the Lord thy God shall bless thee in the land whither thou goest to possess it."*

Deuteronomy 5:29, *" O that there were such an heart in them, that they would fear me, and keep all my commandments always, that it might be well with them, and with their children for ever!"*

Job 10:12, *"Thou hast granted me life and favour, and thy visitation hath preserved my spirit."*

Job 5:26, *"Thou shalt come to thy grave in a full age, like as a shock of corn cometh in his season."*

Job 11:17, *"And thine age shall be clearer than the noonday; thou shalt shine forth, thou shalt be as the morning."*

Psalms 71:17,18, *"O God, thou hast taught me from my youth: and hitherto have I declared thy wondrous works. Now also when I am old and gray headed, O God, forsake me not; until I have shewed thy strength unto this generation, and thy power to everyone that is to come."*

Psalms 71:9, *"Cast me not off in the time of old age; forsake me not when my strength faileth."*

Proverbs 17:22, *"A merry heart doeth good like a medicine; but a broken spirit drieth the bones."*

Psalms 91:16, *"With long life will I satisfy him, and shew him My salvation."*

Psalms 18:2, *"The Lord is my rock, and my fortress, and my deliverer; my God, my strength, in whom I will trust; my buckler, and the horn of my salvation, and my high tower."*

Psalms 22:24, *"For He hath not despised nor abhorred the affliction of the afflicted; neither hath He hid His face from Him; but when he cried unto Him, He heard."*

Nahum 1:7, *"The Lord is good, a stronghold in the day of trouble; and He knoweth them that trust in Him."*

Psalms 37:39, *"But the salvation of the righteous is of the Lord: He is their strength in the time of trouble."*

Matthew 11:28, *"Come unto me, all ye that labour and are heavy laden, and I will give you rest."*

II Corinthians 1:5, *"For as the sufferings of Christ abound in us, so our consolation also aboundeth by Christ."*

Lamentations 3:33, *"For he doth not afflict willingly nor grieve the children of men."*

Psalms 55:22, *"Cast thy burden upon the Lord, and He shall sustain thee: He shall never suffer the righteous to be moved."*

Psalms 9:9, *"The Lord also will be a refuge for the oppressed, a refuge in times of trouble."*

Psalms 28:7, "The Lord is my strength and my shield; my heart trusted in Him, and I am helped: therefore my heart greatly rejoiceth; and with my song will I praise him."

Make good choices; stay focused on the LORD and on His Word. If you feel overwhelmed, saddened or feel yourself becoming depressed, read the Depression, Oppression chapter, and pray the Depression prayer. There you will find wonderfully encouraging scriptures also, to stand on and to claim.

My prayers will be with you as you fight this good fight of faith. May God's grace, mercy, blessings, and His healing virtue be with you at all times. Remember always that,

"...His compassions fail not. They are new every morning: great is thy faithfulness." **Lamentations 3:22,23.**

James 5:14-16, *"Is any sick among you? Let him call for the elders of the church; and let them pray over him, anointing him with oil in the name of the Lord: And the prayer of faith shall save the sick, and the Lord shall raise him up; and if he have committed sins, they shall be forgiven him. Confess your faults one to another, and pray one for another, that ye may be healed. The effectual fervent prayer of a righteous man availeth much."*

Psalms 107:20, ***"He sent His Word, and healed them, and delivered them from their destructions."***

JOEL 3:21, ***"FOR I WILL CLEANSE THEIR BLOOD THAT I HAVE NOT CLEANSED: FOR THE LORD DWELLETH IN ZION."***

Leviticus 17:11, *"For the life of the flesh is in the blood:"*

Ezekiel 16:6, ***"And when I passed by thee, and saw thee polluted in thine own blood, I said unto thee when thou wast in thy blood, Live: yea, I said unto thee when thou wast in thy blood, Live."***

Isaiah 3:10, *"Say ye to the righteous, that it shall be well with him: for they shall eat the fruit of their doings."*
Matthew 15:13, *"But He answered and said, every plant, which my heavenly Father hath not planted, shall be rooted up."* (THIS SCRIPTURE IS GOOD TO STAND ON AGAINST CANCER.)

Job 33:25, *"His flesh shall be fresher than a child's: he shall return to the days of his youth;"* (A GOOD SCRIPTURE TO USE AGAINST CANCER, AND ALL SKIN AND FLESH DISORDERS.)

Psalms 103:3, 4, *"Who forgiveth all thine iniquities; who healeth all thine diseases, Who redeemeth thy life from destruction; who crowneth thee with loving kindness and tender mercies;"*

Psalms 34:19,20, *"Many are the afflictions of the righteous: but the Lord delivereth him out of them all."*

Isaiah 40:29, 31, *"He giveth power to the faint; and to them that have no might He increaseth strength." "But they that wait upon the Lord shall renew their strength; they shall mount up with wings as eagles; they shall run, and not be weary; and they shall walk, and not faint."*

Matthew 9:6-8, *"But that ye know that the Son of man hath power on earth to forgive sins, (then saith He to the sick of the palsy,) Arise, take up thy bed, and go unto thine house. And he arose, and departed to his house. But when the multitudes saw it, they marveled, and glorified God, which had given so much power unto men."*

Joel 3:10, *"Let the weak say, I am strong."*

Jeremiah 30:17, *"For I will restore health unto thee, I will Heal thee of thy wounds, saith the Lord;"*

Matthew 9:15:30,31, *"And great multitudes came unto Him, having with them those that were lame, blind, dumb, maimed, and many others, and cast them down at Jesus' feet; and He healed them: Insomuch that the multitude wondered, when they saw the dumb to speak, the maimed to be whole, the lame to walk, and the blind to see; and they glorified the God of Israel."*

Psalms 25:16-18, *"Turn to me and be gracious to me, for I am lonely and afflicted. The troubles of my heart have multiplied; free* me from my anguish. Look upon my affliction and my distress, and take away all my sins."

Matthew 8:16,17, *"When the even was come they brought unto Him many that were possessed with devils: <u>and He cast out the spirits with His Word, and healed all</u> that were sick: That It might be fulfilled which was spoken by E-sai-as the prophet, saying, Himself took our infirmities, and bare our sicknesses".*

Psalms 128:2, *"For thou shalt eat the labour of thine hands: happy shalt thou be, and it shall be well with thee."*

Luke 4:18, Jesus said, *"The Spirit of the Lord is upon me, because He hath anointed me to preach the gospel to the poor; He hath sent me to heal the brokenhearted, to preach deliverance to the captives, and recovering of sight to the blind, to set at liberty them that are bruised."*

Psalms 139:14, *"I will praise thee, for I am fearfully and wonderfully made: marvelous are thy works; and that, my soul knoweth right well."*

Proverbs 3:7,8, *"Be not wise in thine own eyes: fear the Lord, and depart from evil. It shall be health to thy navel (nerves), and marrow to thy bones."*

Habakkuk 3:19, *"The Lord God is my strength, and He will make my feet like hinds' feet, and He will make me to walk upon mine high places."*

Psalms 91:14,15, *"...therefore will I deliver him: I will set him on high, because he hath known my name. He shall call upon me, and I will answer him: I will be with him in trouble; I will deliver him, and honor him."*

Psalms 91:10-12, *"There shall no evil befall thee, neither shall any plague come nigh thy dwelling. For He shall give his angels charge over thee, to keep thee in all thy ways. They shall bear thee up in their hands, lest thou dash thy foot against a stone."*

Isaiah 12:2, *"Behold, God is my salvation; I will trust, and not be afraid: for the Lord JEHOVAH is my strength and my song; He also is become my salvation."*

Psalms 5:11,12, *"But let all those that put their trust in thee rejoice: let them ever shout for joy, because thou defendest them: let them also that love thy name be joyful in thee. For* thou, Lord, wilt bless the righteous; with favour wilt thou compass him as with a shield."

Job 22:27, *"Thou shalt make thy prayer unto Him, and He shall hear thee…"*

Psalms 9:10, "And they that know thy name will put their trust in thee: for thou, Lord, hast not forsaken them that seek thee."

Romans 8:32, *"He that spared not His own Son, but delivered Him up for us all, how shall He not with Him also freely give us all things."*

Psalms 146:8, "The Lord openeth the eyes of the blind: the Lord raiseth them that are bowed down: the Lord loveth the righteous;"

Psalms 18:32, 33, 36, "It is God that girdeth me with strength, and maketh my way perfect. He maketh my feet like hinds' feet, and setteth me upon my high places." "Thou hast enlarged my steps under me, that my feet did not slip."

James 5:16, *"Confess your faults one to another, and pray one for another, that ye may be healed. The effectual fervent prayer of a righteous man availeth much."*

Psalms 3:3, "But thou, O Lord, art a shield for me; my glory, and the lifter up of my head."

Psalms 138:7, 8, "Though I walk in the midst of trouble, thou wilt revive me: thou shalt stretch forth thine hand against the wrath of mine enemies, and thy right hand shall save me. The Lord will perfect that which concerneth me: thy mercy, Oh Lord, endureth forever: forsake not the works of thine own hands."

Psalms 1:3, "And he shall be like a tree planted by the rivers of water, that bringeth forth his fruit in his season; his leaf also shall not wither; and whatsoever he doeth shall prosper."

Matthew 21:22, "And all things, whatsoever ye shall ask in prayer, believing, ye shall receive."

II Tim.1:7, "For God hath not given us the spirit of fear; but of power, and of love, and of a sound mind."

Mark 16:17,18, *"And these signs shall follow them that believe: In my name shall they cast out devils; they shall speak with new* tongues; If they drink any deadly thing, it shall not hurt them; they shall lay hands on the sick and they shall recover."

Isaiah 58:11, *"And the Lord shall guide thee continually, and satisfy thy soul in drought, and make fat thy bones: and thou shalt be like a watered garden, and like a spring of water, whose waters fail not."*

Habakkuk 2:2, *"And the Lord answered me, and said, Write the vision, and make it plain upon tables, that He may run that readeth it."*

Psalms 107:20, *"He sent His Word, and healed them, and delivered them from their destructions."*

I John 5:14-15, *"And this is the confidence that we have in him, that, if we ask any thing according to His will, He heareth us: And if we know that He hear us, whatsoever we ask, we know that we have the petitions that we desired of Him."*

3 John 1:2, *"Beloved, I wish above all things that thou mayest prosper and be in health, even as thy soul prospereth."*

John 16: 23, 24, *"....Whatsoever ye shall ask the Father in my name, He will give it you" "... ask, and ye shall receive, that your joy may be full."*

Matthew 15:30,31, *"And great multitudes came unto Him, having with them those that were lame, blind, dumb, maimed, and many others, and cast them down at Jesus' feet; and He healed them. Insomuch that the multitude wondered, when they saw the dumb speak, the maimed to be whole, the lame to walk, and the blind to see: and they glorified the God of Israel."*

Ecclesiastes 3:13, *"And also that every man should eat and drink, and enjoy the good of all his labour, it is the gift of God."*

Jeremiah 29:12, *"Then shall ye call upon me, and ye shall go and pray unto me, and I will hearken unto you."*

Jesus wants to heal your body; He has given us the tools that we need to receive our healing and to defeat the enemy. Do not be deceived; you really do have an enemy and you really do have to fight, to defeat him. If your body has been assaulted with a serious disease of any kind, like cancer, heart disease, and so many other things, you must fight! You must fight to win! Praise God, he has equipped us with everything that we need to be victorious. We are God's instruments on earth, and we have to take up our sword, and our shield; we have to put His Words in our mouths, and fight!

Jesus defeated Satan and all his demons on the cross, and has given us His Holy Spirit, the Holy Ghost, to enable us with overcoming power. He has given us power over all the power of the enemy. We have to stand against Satan and every demon from the pit of hell; we have to use the power that Jesus gave us to defeat him. We have to agree with God's Words, speak God's Words, and stand on God's Words. If we believe in our heavenly Father, have faith, and declare His Words over our lives, He will do miracles in our lives.

God loves us, we are His children. When we have faith in God, and in His Word, take out our Sword, and fight the enemy, He will do His part. He will perform the miracle that we need. We need to claim whatsoever we need, and want. He never fails, and His grace is always sufficient.

Romans 8:2, "*For the law of the Spirit of life in Christ Jesus hath made me free from the law of sin and death.*" Claim God's law of the Spirit of life operating in your body and in your mind. Claim God's promises over your life. Declare that, "*I shall not die, but live and declare the works of the Lord*!" Claim God's promises, declare God's promises and believe God's promises. Have Faith in God. We have a covenant with God, who promises our healing. Claim It! Believe it! Stand on it!

The very same Spirit that raised Christ from the dead lives in you! Declare your healing. Declare God's quickening Spirit at work, totally restoring your body. Pray your healing scriptures over and over, many times a day, if possible. Trust in, and give praise to God. Place upon your body a garment of praise. Praise God for all of His promises. Thank your heavenly Father, that all of His promises to you are yes, and Amen in Christ Jesus. Trust in your Saviour.

The Word tells us to choose this day, life or death, blessings or curses. Choose life that you may live. Choose God's blessings over your life. Thank Him that His quickening power is at work in your body; restoring your RNA, and your DNA; restoring every fiber of your being, perfecting, and creatively restoring you now.

Jeremiah 30:17 tells us, "*For I will restore health unto thee, and I will heal thee of thy wounds, saith the Lord;*"

Thank Him that your body is getting stronger every minute of the day and night. Speak life over your body; speak peace over your body. Call forth the miracle working power of Jesus into your body. Call forth the Spirit of life- God's quickening Spirit- to restore your entire body. Call forth the abundant life that we might have because Christ came. Thank God for His Word! Speak His Word; His Word is life to all your flesh!

Romans 8:11, *"But if the Spirit of Him that raised up Jesus from the dead dwell in you, He that raised up Christ from the dead shall also quicken your mortal bodies by His Spirit that dwelleth in you."* Thank God that His quickening Spirit is raising up your body to full restoration; the same Spirit that raised up Christ from the dead.

Psalms 30:2,3, *"O Lord my God, I cried unto thee, and thou hast healed me. Oh Lord, thou hast brought up my soul from the grave: thou hast kept me alive, that I should not go down to the pit."* Thank Him; sing unto Him, Praise and Magnify His Holy name!

Isaiah 35:3, *"Strengthen ye the weak hands, and confirm the feeble knees."*

Matthew 9:18,23-26, *"...there came a certain ruler, and worshipped Him, saying, My daughter is even now dead: but come and lay thy hand upon her, and she shall live. And when Jesus came into the ruler's house, and saw the minstrels and the people making a noise, He said unto them. Give place: for the maid is not dead, but sleepeth. And they laughed Him to scorn. But when the people were put forth, He went in, and took her by the hand, and the maid arose. And the fame hereof went abroad into all that land."*

Psalms 118:14, *"The Lord is my strength and song, and is become my salvation."*

Acts 10:38, *"How God anointed Jesus of Nazareth with the Holy Ghost and with power: who went about doing good, and healing all that were oppressed of the devil; for God was with Him."*

I THANK YOU, FATHER, THAT I AM RECEIVING ALL OF THE BENEFITS OF YOUR WORD. I LOOSE THE ANOINTING OF GOD'S QUICKENING SPIRIT TO TOTALLY HEAL AND RESTORE MY MIND, BODY, SOUL AND SPIRIT. I LOOSE THE

ANOINTING OF THE HEALING VIRTUE OF JESUS CHRIST, AND THE POWER IN ALL OF THESE HEALING SCRIPTURES OVER ME, FROM THE TOP OF MY HEAD, TO THE SOLES OF MY FEET, IN JESUS' NAME, AMEN.

NOTES

Part VI. Depression and Oppression

Chapter Eleven
Teaching on Depression

Webster's defines depression as "a state of feeling sad: dejection: a psychoneurotic or psychotic disorder marked by sadness, inactivity and self-depreciation: a reduction in activity, amount, quality or force."

A state of depression always starts in one's mind. As children of God, we must recognize depression for what it is- a trick of the enemy to gain access through our minds, into our souls and into our bodies.

Ephesians 6:10-13, *"Finally, my brethren, be strong in the Lord, and in the power of His might. Put on the whole armor of God, that ye may be able to stand against the wiles* (the strategies) *of the devil. For we wrestle not against flesh and blood, but against principalities, against powers, against the rulers of the darkness of this world, against spiritual wickedness in high places. Wherefore take unto you the whole armor of God, that ye may be able to withstand in the evil day, and having done all, to stand."*

In **Ephesians 6:11-18**, we are told how to put on the whole armor of God. We should put on this armor every morning, along with our blood protection, totally encapsulating ourselves with the blood of Jesus. We saturate every cell, every fiber of our being, in Jesus' name, for our total protection and safety this day and night. When we have on the whole armor of God, and our blood protection, in Jesus' name, we are strong in the Lord, and in the power of His might, and, we are able to stand against the wiles of the devil.

Depression is an insidious, direct attack of the devil, which allows him to have his way in our minds. Depression allows him to gain control over not only our minds, but also our hearts and bodies. Webster's defines the word insidious as, "an ambush: awaiting a chance to entrap: treacherous: harmful but enticing: seductive: having a gradual and cumulative effect: developing so gradually as to be well established before becoming apparent." Talk about a sneaky, deceitful devil, which tries to trick our minds in so many ways. Attacks against our minds certainly qualify as insidious. You may have heard of cancer, or another dreaded disease being described as insidious; this is because one may not realize that they have a problem, until it is full blown.

When we are faced with any type of disease, including cancer, or heart disease, we should realize that we need to take responsibility for our physical problem- quickly! We have to rebuke and bind Satan away from our bodies and our minds; plead the blood of Jesus over ourselves; and loose, declare that which we want, in Jesus' name, and stand on the Word of God. We are also to call for the elders of the church, and have them pray over us in obedience to **James 5:13-15.** *"Is any among you afflicted? Let him pray. Is any merry? Let him sing Psalms. Is any sick among you? let him call for the elders of the church; and let them pray over him, anointing him with oil in the name of the Lord: And the prayer of faith shall save the sick, and the Lord shall raise him up: and if he have committed sins, they shall be forgiven him."*

It is also a good thing to have a friend, someone with whom to be a prayer partner, to hold you up daily before God. After one has aggressively attacked, and bound Satan away from them, the enemy will try to come back with his subtleties.

After praying, we should do according to **Proverbs 4:20-22,** *"My son, attend to My Words; incline thine ear unto my sayings. Let them not depart from thine eyes; keep them in the midst of thine heart. For they are life unto those that find them, and health to all their flesh."* When we are attending to God's Words, keeping them in front of our eyes by reading them, and in the midst of our hearts by thinking on them, we haven't time to think on negative things.

Thank God, my mother taught me at an early age not to listen to the devil and allow him to make me depressed. She told me, "You can't keep bad thoughts from coming into your mind sometimes...but you can certainly keep them from roosting, or staying there." She compared bad thoughts to a nasty, old filthy buzzard. She told me, "When bad thoughts come into your mind, realize that God didn't put them there. You know the devil put them there; so when they come, rebuke, and bind them away from you, in Jesus' name. Just scare them away, like you would an old buzzard." She also told me to, "sweep bad thoughts out of your mind, like you would sweep dirt out of your house. Don't allow them to stay because they grow like fuzz balls, and become strongholds in your life. Just sweep away like dirt, all bad thoughts." Because of following her lead in this area, I learned at an early age not to let negative, bad thoughts dominate my thinking. When bad thoughts come to me, I say, "NO devil, I rebuke you, and tell you to flee in Jesus' name" and follow that up with a scripture, such as the ones below, and he has to leave.

Psalms 94:11, tells us that, *"...The Lord knoweth the thoughts of man."*

Proverbs 16:3, tells us to, *"Commit thy works unto the Lord, and thy thoughts shall be established."*

Jeremiah 29:11, *"For I know the thoughts that I think toward you, saith the Lord, thoughts of peace, and not of evil, to give you an expected end."* Let's be spiritually minded so we will have life and peace as in **Romans 8:6,** *"For to be carnally minded is death; but to be spiritually minded is life and peace."* Paul tells us in **II Timothy 1:7,** *"For God hath not given us the spirit of fear; but of power, and of love, and of a sound mind."* Let's think ourselves happy, like Paul told King Agrippa in *Acts 26:2, "I think myself happy,"* *Think* about it! Try it! <u>**THINK YOURSELF HAPPY!**</u>

In **Isaiah 14:24,** we learn that, *"The Lord of hosts hath sworn, saying, Surely as I have thought, so shall it come to pass: and as I have purposed, so shall it stand."* Our thoughts, along with our words, are powerful. Let's make sure that we use them to accomplish good, positive, rewarding, and fulfilling things in our lives. We have God's magnificent Words, the scriptures, to think on, and to stand on. Let's feed our minds with them, speak them out our mouths, claim them, stand, and praise God that they are becoming realities in our lives. **Psalms 139:17,18,** *"How precious also are thy thoughts unto me, O God! How great is the sum of them! If I should count them, they are more in number than the sand:"* What a wonderful, reassuring scripture, that <u>God's thoughts towards us are more than the grains of sand</u>. Praise His Holy name!

Proverbs 15:23, *"A man hath joy by the answer of his mouth: and a Word spoken in due season, how good is it!"*

Proverbs 17:22, *"A merry heart doeth good like a medicine."* Thank God, we have joy when we speak God's Words with our mouths. God's Words doeth us good, like a medicine, and maketh our hearts merry.

Psalms 16:11, *"Thou wilt shew me the path of life: in thy presence is fullness of joy; at thy right hand there are pleasures for evermore!"*

Psalms 5:11,12, *"But let all those that put their trust in Thee rejoice: let them ever shout for joy, because thou defendest them: let them also that love thy name be joyful in thee. For thou, Lord, wilt bless the righteous; with favor wilt thou compass him as with a shield."*

Psalms 107:20, *"He sent His Word, and healed them, and delivered them from their destructions."*

Isaiah 53:4, 5, *"Surely he hath borne our grief's, and carried our sorrows: yet we did esteem Him stricken, smitten of God, and afflicted. But he was wounded for our transgressions, He was bruised for our iniquities: the chastisement of our peace was upon Him; and with His stripes we are healed."*

Romans 8:2,4- 6, *"For the law of the Spirit of life in Christ Jesus hath made me free from the law of sin and death." "That the righteousness of the law might be fulfilled in us, who walk not after the flesh, but after the Spirit. For they that are after the flesh do mind the things of the flesh; but they that are after the Spirit the Things of the Spirit. For to be carnally minded is death; but to be Spiritually minded is life and peace."*

Philippians 4:6-9, *"Be careful for nothing; but in everything by prayer and supplication with thanksgiving let your requests be made known unto God. And the peace of God, which passeth all understanding, shall keep your hearts and minds through Christ Jesus. Finally brethren, whatsoever things are true, whatsoever things are honest, whatsoever things are just, whatsoever things are pure, whatsoever things are lovely, whatsoever things are of good report; if there be any virtue, and if there be any praise, think on these things. Those things, which ye have both learned, and received, and heard, and seen in me, do: and the God of peace shall be with you."*

Romans 14:17,19, *"For the Kingdom of God is not meat and drink; but righteousness, and peace, and joy in the Holy Ghost."* *"Therefore follow after the things which make for peace, and things wherewith one may edify another."*

Joshua 1:9, *"Have not I commanded thee? Be strong and of a good courage; be not afraid, neither be thou dismayed: for the Lord thy God is with thee whithersoever thou goest."*

Take wonderful, uplifting scriptures and your prayers with you wherever you go. You can read them, think on, and claim them, anytime you feel depression, or oppression trying to overtake you.

Go through all the scriptures in the prayer for Depression and Oppression, and the scriptures following the prayer. Also, go through Psalms and Proverbs, choosing scriptures that speak to you. Put the scriptures on tape to listen to, or on 3 x 5 cards, and memorize them. Put them in your mind, and in your heart, and think on these things. Declare your healing and your joy, in Jesus' name. The anointing shows up when you are joyful, and the anointing breaks the yolk, according to **Isaiah 10:27,** <u>SPEAK GOD'S WORDS! THEY RELEASE GOD'S POWER... AND THEY WORK</u>!

<u>Notes</u>

Prayer of Release
From Depression and Oppression

I bind Satan, the prince of the air, and all evil spirits away from me, and cast them into outer darkness. I bind all assignments from every evil source; assignments of sadness, dejection, suppression, depression, oppression, terror, distress, self-pity, discouragement, and fear. I say to all evil assignments against me, be thou removed, and be thou cast into the sea, according to **Mark 11:23.** I plead the blood of Jesus over me, from the top of my head to my toes, and ask that you fill all voids, Lord, with the blood of Jesus. I am established in your righteousness, oh God, through Christ Jesus.

No evil spirits, or their assignments, shall come near me. I am complete in Him, who spoiled all principality, and power, and made a show of them openly. **Colossians 2:13-15**, *"And you, being dead in your sins and the uncircumcision of your flesh, hath He quickened together with him, having forgiven you all trespasses: Blotting out the handwriting of ordinances that was against us, which was contrary to us, and took it out of the way, nailing it to His cross. And having spoiled principalities and powers, He made a shew of them openly, triumphing over them in it."* and in **Galations 3:13-15**, *"Christ hath redeemed us from the curse of the law, being made a curse for us: for it is written, Cursed is everyone that hangeth on a tree. That the blessing of Abraham might come on the Gentiles through Jesus Christ; that we might receive the promise of the Spirit through faith."*

I thank you, God, that you are the strength of my heart, mind, soul, and spirit; Thank you for a spirit of love, and for a calm, peaceful, orderly, balanced mind, a renewed Spirit, mind, and body.

II Timothy 1:7, *"For God hath not given us the spirit of fear; but of power, and of love, and of a sound mind."* **I Corinthians 2:16**, *"For who hath known the mind of the Lord, that he may instruct him? But we have the mind of Christ."* And the peace of God, which passeth all understanding, shall keep your hearts and minds through Christ Jesus.

Job 10:12, *"Thou hast granted me life and favour, and thy visitation hath preserved my spirit."*

I LOOSE THE ANOINTING OF GOD, AND THE POWER IN ALL OF THESE WONDERFUL SCRIPTURES INTO MY MIND, HEART AND SOUL, TO STRENGTHEN, AND TO MAKE ME JOYOUS IN EVERY WAY. I THANK YOU, FATHER, FOR ALL OF THESE BENEFITS AND BLESSINGS, WHICH YOU ARE IMPARTING INTO MY LIFE, IN JESUS' NAME I PRAY, AND GIVE THANKS, AMEN.

NOTES

Scriptures To Stand on
Against Depression and Oppression

Acts10:38, *"How God anointed Jesus of Nazareth with the Holy Ghost and with power: who went about doing good,* **and healing all that were oppressed** *of the devil; for God was with Him."*

Romans 8:11, ***"But if the Spirit of Him that raised up Jesus from the dead dwell in you; He that raised up Christ from the dead shall also quicken your mortal bodies   by His Spirit that dwelleth in you."***

II Timothy 1:7, *"For God hath not given us the spirit of fear; but of power, and of love, and of a sound mind."*

Proverbs 15:23, *"A man hath joy by the answer of his mouth: and a word spoken in due season, how good is it."*

Proverbs 15:30, "The light of the eyes rejoiceth the heart: and a good report maketh the bones fat."

Proverbs 16:24, *"Pleasant words are as an honeycomb, sweet to the soul, and health to the bones."*

Psalms 34:4, *"I sought the Lord, and He heard me, and delivered me from all my fears."*

Psalms 34:7, *"The angel of the Lord encampeth round about them that fear him, and delivereth them."*

Isaiah 26:3, *"Thou wilt keep him in perfect peace, whose mind is stayed on thee: because he trusteth in thee."*

Proverbs 3:24, *"When thou liest down, thou shalt not be afraid: yea, thou shalt lie down, and thy sleep shall be sweet."*

Colossians 1:10,11, *"That ye might walk worthy of the Lord unto all pleasing, being fruitful in every good work, and increasing in the knowledge of God; Strengthened with all might, according to His glorious power, unto all patience and longsuffering with joyfulness."*

Romans 15:13, *"Now the God of hope fill you with all joy and peace in believing, that ye may abound in hope, through the power of the Holy Ghost."*

Psalms 46-1-3, *"God is our refuge and strength, a very present help in trouble. Therefore will not we fear, though the earth be* removed, and though the mountains be carried into the midst of the sea: Though the waters thereof roar and be troubled, though the mountains shake with the swelling thereof."

II Corinthians 5:7, *"For we walk by faith, not by sight:"*

Psalms 18:2, *"The Lord is my rock, and my fortress, and my deliverer; my God, my strength, in whom I will trust; my buckler, and the horn of my salvation, and my high tower."*

Psalms 22:24, *"For He hath not despised nor abhorred the affliction of the afflicted; neither hath He hid His face from him; but when he cried unto Him, He heard."*

Nahum 1:7, *"The Lord is good, a stronghold in the day of trouble; and He knoweth them that trust in Him."*

Psalms 37:39, *"But the salvation of the righteous is of the Lord: He is their strength in the time of trouble."*

Psalms 55:22, *"Cast thy burden upon the Lord, and He shall sustain thee: He shall never suffer the righteous to be moved."*

II Corinthians 1:5, *"For as the sufferings of Christ abound in us, so our consolation also aboundeth by Christ."*

Psalms 9:9, *"The Lord will also be refuge for the oppressed..."*

Psalms 27:14, *"Wait on the Lord: be of good courage, and He shall strengthen thine heart: Wait, I say, on the Lord."*

Proverbs 17:22, "A merry heart doeth good like a medicine; but a broken spirit drieth the bones."*

John 14:27, "Peace I leave with you, my peace I give unto you: not as the world giveth, give I unto you, Let not your heart be troubled, neither let it be afraid."*

Isaiah 54:14, *"In righteousness shalt thou be established: thou shalt be far from oppression; for thou shalt not fear: and from terror; for it shall not come near thee."*

I Peter 5:7, *"Casting all your care upon Him; for He careth for you."*

I Peter 3:12, "For the eyes of the Lord are over the righteous, and His ears are open unto their prayers:"*

Psalms 118:6, *"The Lord is on my side; I will not fear: what can man do unto me?"*

Psalms 118:1, *"O give thanks unto the Lord; for He is good: because His mercy endureth forever."*

John 16:33, *"These things I have spoken unto you, that in me ye might have peace. In the world ye shall have tribulation: but be* *of good cheer; I have overcome the world."*

John 17:8-11, Jesus praying unto the Father said, ***"For I have given unto them the Words which thou gavest me; and they have received them, and have known surely that I came out from thee, and they have believed that thou didst send me. I pray for them: I pray not for the world, but for them, which thou hast given me; for they are thine. And all mine are thine, and thine are mine; and I am glorified in them. And now I am no more in the world, but these are in the world, and I come to thee. Holy Father, keep through thine own name those whom thou hast given me, that they may be one, as we are."***

I John 4:18, *"There is no fear in love; but perfect love casteth out fear: because fear hath torment. He that feareth is not made perfect in love."*

Psalms 107:28,29, *"Then they cry unto the Lord in their trouble, and He bringeth them out of their distresses. He maketh the storm a calm, so that the waves thereof are still."*

Psalms 112: 7,8, *"He shall not be afraid of evil tidings: his heart is fixed, trusting in the Lord. His heart is established, he shall not be afraid, until he see his desire upon his enemies."*

Psalms 119:165, *"Great peace have they which love thy law: and nothing shall offend them."*

Psalms 46:11, *"The Lord of hosts is with us; the God of Jacob is our refuge. Selah."*

Isaiah 40:29,31, *"He giveth power to the faint: and to them that have no might He increaseth strength." "But they that wait upon the Lord shall renew their strength; they shall mount up with wings as eagles; they shall run, and not be weary; and they shall walk, and not faint."*

Isaiah 43:1, *"...Fear not, for I have redeemed thee, I have called thee by thy name, thou art mine."*

Isaiah 41:10, *"Fear thou not; for I am with thee: be not dismayed; for I am thy God: I will strengthen thee; yea, I will help thee; yea, I will uphold thee with the right hand of my righteousness."*

PART VII. Miscellaneous Prayer

Chapter Twelve
Protection Prayer

Please pray your Daily Prayer, including putting on the whole armor of God, bind Satan and all evil, before praying the Protection Prayer.

Dear Heavenly Father, I boldly come before your throne to ask for protection of my spouse, children, pastors, our family members, and myself. Father, I seek your peace, your welfare, your deliverance and protection for each of us. In this request, and in everything by prayer and petition, with thanksgiving, I make my wants known to you. Help each of us to acknowledge you always, so that you will direct our paths, to fear you, and to forever depart from evil. *"Order my steps in thy Word: and let not any iniquity have dominion over me. Deliver me from the oppression of man: so will I keep thy precepts."* **Psalms 119:133, 134.**

I thank you, Father, for all the angels you have given unto us, to watch over us, and to keep us from harm. I loose them now, our guardian, bidding angels, and all the angels of the Lord, to come forth, and keep each of us from all harm, lest we dash our foot against a stone.

We are victorious over all principalities, powers, rulers of the darkness of this world, and spiritual wickedness in high places, where ever we are, at all times. Greater is He that is within us, than he, that is within the world.

I declare that *"No weapon that is formed against thee shall prosper,"* **Isaiah 54:17**, and every thing we do shall prosper. *"But the salvation of the righteous is of the Lord: He is their strength in the time of trouble. And the Lord shall help them, and deliver them: He shall deliver them from the wicked, and save them, because they trust in him,"* **Psalms 37:39, 40**

We are told in **Psalms 91:10-12,** *"There shall no evil befall thee, neither shall any plague come nigh thy dwelling. For He shall give His angels charge over thee, to keep thee in all thy ways. They shall bear thee up in their hands, lest thou dash* *thy foot against a stone."* I thank you, *"For God hath not given us a spirit of fear; but of power, and of love, and of a sound mind."* II Timothy 1:7.

I loose the power, and the Anointing of God, for complete, total protection for each of us, over our businesses, occupations, and possessions, day and night. I ask for the blood of Jesus to speak continually for us, for total protection, in the name of Jesus Christ, and according to the Word of God. I loose the power in all of these scriptures over each of us, our properties, and possessions. I thank you Father, for the manifestation of the very best outcome for each of us, in all situations; and for the extreme favor of God, and of man, that is continually over us. Amen.

NOTES

Protection Scriptures

Luke 10:19, *"Behold, I give unto you power to tread upon serpents and scorpions, and over all the power of the enemy: and nothing shall by any means hurt you:"*

Joshua 1:5,9, *"There shall not any man be able to stand before thee all the days of thy life; as I was with Moses, so I will be with thee: I will not fail thee, nor forsake thee."* *"Have not I commanded thee? Be strong and of a good courage; be not afraid, neither be thou dismayed; for the Lord thy God is with thee whithersoever thou goest."*

Deuteronomy 33:25-27,29, *"Thy shoes shall be iron and brass: and as thy days, so shall thy strength be. There is none like unto the God of Jeshrun, who rideth upon the heaven in thy help, and in His Excellency on the sky. The eternal God is thy refuge, and underneath are the everlasting arms: and He shall thrust out the enemy from before thee, and shall say, Destroy them."* *"Happy art thou, O Israel: who is like unto thee; O people saved by the Lord, the shield of thy help, and who is the sword of thy Excellency! And thine enemies shall be found liars unto thee; and thou shalt tread upon their high places."*

Psalms 46:1, 2, *"God is our refuge and strength, a very present help in trouble. Therefore will not we fear, though the earth be removed, and though the mountains be carried into the midst of the sea;"*

Psalms 46:7, *"The Lord of Hosts is with us; the God of Jacob is our refuge. Sela".*

Jeremiah 29:11, *"For I know the thoughts that I think toward you, saith the Lord, thoughts of peace, and not of evil, to give you an expected end."*

Psalms 129:4, 5, *"The Lord is righteous: He hath cut asunder the cords of the wicked. Let them all be confounded and turned back that hate Zion."*

Psalms 94:22, 23, *"But the Lord is my defense; and my God is the rock of my refuge. And He shall bring upon them their own iniquity, and shall cut them off in their own wickedness; yea, the Lord shall cut them off."*

Isaiah 54:15, *"...whosoever shall gather together against thee* *shall fall for thy sake."*

Psalms 33:10, *"The Lord bringeth the counsel of the heathen to nought: he maketh the devices of the people of none effect."*

Job 11:17-19, *"And thine age shall be clearer than the noonday: thou shalt shine forth, thou shalt be as the morning. And thou shalt be secure, because there is hope; yea, thou shalt dig about thee, and thou shalt take thy rest in safety. Also thou shalt lie down and none shall make thee afraid;"*

Romans 8:2, *"For the Law of the Spirit of life in Christ Jesus hath made me free from the law of sin and death."*

Psalms 138:7, 8, *"Though I walk in the midst of trouble thou wilt revive me: thou shalt stretch forth thine hand against the wrath of mine enemies, and thy right hand shall save me. The Lord will perfect that which concerneth me: thy mercy, oh Lord, endureth forever: forsake not the works of thine own hands."*

Deuteronomy *28:7,* *"The Lord shall cause thine enemies that rise up against thee to be smitten before thy face; they shall come out against thee one way, and flee before thee seven ways."*

Deuteronomy 3:22, *"Ye shall not fear them; for the Lord your God He shall fight for you."*

Luke 18:7, *"And shall not God avenge His own elect, which cry day and night unto Him, though He bear long with them?"*

Proverbs 21:1, *"The king's heart is in the hand of the Lord, as the rivers of water: He turneth it whithersoever He will."*

Psalms 7:10, *"My defense is of God, which saveth the upright in heart."*

Proverbs 3:26, *"For the Lord shall be thy confidence, and shall keep thy foot from being taken."*

Psalms 3:3, *"But thou, O Lord, art a shield for me; my glory, and the lifter up of my head."*

Isaiah 41:11,12, *"Behold, all they that were incensed against thee shall be ashamed and confounded: they shall be as nothing; and they that strive with thee shall perish. Thou shalt seek them, and shalt not find them, even them that contended with thee: they that war against thee shall be as nothing; and as a thing of nought."*

Psalms 16:5, *"The Lord is the portion of mine inheritance and of my cup: thou maintainest my lot."* (He guards all that is mine)

Psalms 97:10, *"Ye that love the Lord, hate evil: He preserveth the souls of His saints; He delivereth them out of the hand of the* *wicked."*

Psalms 1:3, *"And he shall be like a tree planted by the rivers of water, that bringeth forth his fruit in his season; his leaf also shall not wither; and whatsoever he doeth shall prosper."*

Hebrews 13:6, *"So that we may boldly say, The Lord is my helper, and I will not fear what man shall do unto me."*

Deuteronomy 33:7, *"...and this is the blessing of Judah, let his hands be sufficient for him; and be thou an help to him from his enemies."*

Psalms 91:10-12, *"There shall no evil befall thee, neither shall any plague come nigh thy dwelling. For He shall give His angels charge over thee, to keep thee in all thy ways. They shall bear thee up in their hands, lest thou dash thy foot against a stone."*

Proverbs 3:25, 26, *"Be not afraid of sudden fear, neither of the desolation of the wicked, when it cometh. For the Lord shall be thy confidence, and shall keep thy foot from being taken."*

Psalms 5:11,12, *"But let all those that put their trust in thee rejoice: let them ever shout for joy, because thou defendest them: let them also that love thy name be joyful in thee. For thou, Lord, wilt bless the righteous; with favor wilt thou compass him as with a shield."*

Isaiah 8:10, *"Take counsel together, and it shall come to naught; speak the Word, and it shall not stand; for God is with us."*

II Kings 6:16, *"And he answered, Fear not: for they that be with us are more than they that be with them."*

II Timothy 4:18, *"And the Lord shall deliver me from every evil work, and will preserve me unto His heavenly Kingdom:"*

Psalms 25:10, *"All the paths of the Lord are mercy and truth unto such as keep His covenant and His testimonies."*

II Chronicles 20:15, *"...Be not afraid, nor dismayed by reason of this great multitude; for the battle is not yours, but God's."*

Acts 18:10, *"For I am with thee, and no man shall set on thee to hurt thee: for I have much people in this city."*

Nahum 1:7, *"The Lord is good, a strong hold in the day of trouble; and He knoweth them that trust in Him "*

John 16:33, *"These things I have spoken unto you, that in me ye might have peace. In the world ye shall have tribulation: but be of good cheer; I have overcome the world."*

Psalms 9:9, *"The Lord also will be a refuge for the oppressed, a refuge in times of trouble."*

Proverbs11:21, *"Though hand join in hand, the wicked shall not be unpunished: but the seed of the righteous shall be delivered."*

Psalms 41:11,12, *"By this I know that thou favourest me, because mine enemy doth not triumph over me. And as for me, thou upholdest me in mine integrity, and settest me before thy face for ever."*

Psalms 46:1-3, *"God is our refuge and strength, a very present help in trouble. Therefore will not we fear, though the earth be removed, and though the mountains be carried into the midst of the sea: Though the waters thereof roar and be troubled, though the mountains shake with the swelling thereof."*

Psalms 18:2, *"The Lord is my rock, and my fortress, and my deliverer; my God, my strength, in whom I will trust; my buckler, and the horn of my salvation, and my high tower."*

Psalms 33:10, *"The Lord bringeth the counsel of the heathen to nought: He maketh the devices of the people of none effect."*

Psalms 34:7- 9, *"The angel of the Lord encampeth round about them that fear Him, and delivereth them. O taste and see that the Lord is good: blessed is the man that trusteth in Him. O fear the Lord, ye His saints: for there is no want to them that fear Him."*

Psalms 37:39, *"But the salvation of the righteous is of the Lord: He is their strength in the time of trouble."*

Psalms 55:22, *"Cast thy burden upon the Lord, and He shall sustain thee: He shall never suffer the righteous to be moved."*

Luke 10:19, *"Behold, I give unto you power to tread upon serpents and scorpions, and over all the power of the enemy: and nothing shall by any means hurt you."*

Psalms 23:1-6, *"The Lord is my shepherd; I shall not want. He maketh me to lie down in green pastures: He leadeth me beside the still waters. He restoreth my soul: He leadeth me in the paths of righteousness for His name's sake. Yea, though I walk through the valley of the shadow of death, I will fear no evil: for thou art with me; thy rod and thy staff they comfort me. Thou preparest a table before me in the presence of mine enemies: thou anointest my head with oil; my cup runneth* *over. Surely goodness and mercy shall follow me all the days of my life: and I will dwell in the house of the Lord for ever."*

Psalms 27, *"The Lord is my light and my salvation; whom shall I fear? The Lord is the strength of my life; of whom shall I be afraid? When the wicked, even mine enemies and my foes, came upon me to eat up my flesh, they stumbled and fell. Though an host should encamp against me, my heart shall not fear: though war should rise against me, in this will I be confident. One thing have I desired of the Lord, that will I seek after: that I may dwell in the house of the Lord all the days of my life, to behold the beauty of the Lord, and to inquire in His temple. For in the time of trouble He shall hide me in His pavilion: in the secret of His tabernacle shall He hide me; He shall set me up upon a rock. And now shall mine head be lifted up above mine enemies round about me: therefore will I offer in His tabernacle sacrifices of joy; I will sing, yea, I will sing praises unto the Lord. Hear, O Lord, when I cry with my voice: have mercy also upon me, and answer me. When thou saidst, Seek ye my face; my heart said unto thee, Thy face, Lord, will I seek. Hide not thy face far from me; put not thy servant away in anger: thou hast been my help; leave me not, neither forsake me, O God of my salvation. When my father and my mother forsake me, then the Lord will take me up. Teach me thy way, O Lord, and lead me in a plain path, because of mine enemies. Deliver me not over unto the will of mine enemies; for false witnesses are risen up against me, and such as breath out cruelty. I had fainted, unless I had believed to see the goodness of the Lord in the land of the living. Wait on the Lord: be of good courage, and He shall strengthen thine heart: wait, I say, on the Lord."*

Psalms 91:1-16, *"He that dwelleth in the secret place of the most High shall abide under the shadow of the Almighty. I will say of the Lord, He is my refuge and my fortress: my God; in Him will I trust. Surely He shall deliver thee from the snare of the fowler, and from the noisome pestilence. He shall cover thee with His feathers, and under His wings shalt thou trust: His truth shall be thy shield and buckler. Thou shalt not be afraid for the terror by night; nor for the arrow that flieth by day; Nor for the pestilence that walketh in darkness; nor for the destruction that wasteth at noonday. A thousand shall fall at thy side, and ten thousand at thy right hand;*

but it shall not come nigh thee. Only with thine eyes shalt thou behold and see the reward of the wicked. Because thou hast made the Lord, which is my refuge, even the most High, thy habitation; There shall no evil befall thee, neither shall any plague come nigh thy dwelling. For He shall give His angels charge over thee, to keep thee in all thy ways. They shall bear thee up in their hands, lest thou dash thy foot against a stone. Thou shalt tread upon the lion and adder: the young lion and the dragon shalt thou trample under feet. Because He hath set His love upon me, therefore will I deliver him: I will set him on high, because he hath known my name. He shall call upon me, and I will answer him: I will be with him in trouble; I will deliver him, and honour him. With long life will I satisfy him, and shew him my salvation."

Isaiah 43:1,2, **"But now thus saith the Lord that created thee, O Jacob, and He that formed thee, O Israel, Fear not: for I have redeemed thee, I have called thee by thy name; thou art mine. When thou passest through the waters, I will be with thee; and through the rivers, they shall not overflow thee: when thou walkest through the fire, thou shalt not be burned; neither shall the flame kindle upon thee."**

Lamentations 3:33, *"For He doth not afflict willingly nor grieve the children of men."*

Proverbs 18:10, *"The name of the Lord is a strong tower: the righteous runneth into it, and is safe."*

Psalms 138:7, *"Though I walk in the midst of trouble, thou wilt revive me: thou shalt stretch forth thine hand against the wrath of mine enemies, and thy right hand shall save me."*

I Peter 3:13, *"And who is he that will harm you, if ye be followers of that which is good?"*

Psalms 22:24, *"For He hath not despised nor abhorred the affliction of the afflicted; neither hath He hid His face from him; but when he cried unto Him, He heard."*

Job 11:18,19, *"And thou shalt be secure, because there is hope; yea, thou shalt dig about thee, and thou shalt take thy rest in safety. Also thou shalt lie down, and none shall make thee afraid; yea, many shall make suit unto thee."*

Proverbs 3:24, *"When thou liest down, thou shalt not be afraid: yea, thou shalt lie down, and thy sleep shall be sweet."*

Psalms 4:8, *"I will both lay me down in peace, and sleep: for* thou, Lord, only makest me dwell in safety."

Hebrews 13:6, *"So that we may boldly say, The Lord is my helper, and I will not fear what man shall do unto me."*

Psalms 37:24, *"Though he fall, he shall not be utterly cast down: for the Lord upholdeth him with His hand."*

Psalms 18:2, *"The Lord is my rock, and my fortress, and my deliverer; my God, my strength, in whom I will trust; my buckler, and the horn of my salvation, and my high tower."*

Psalms 112:7, *"He shall not be afraid of evil tidings: his heart is fixed, trusting in the Lord."*

Proverbs 1:33, *"But whoso hearkeneth unto me shall dwell safely, and shall be quiet from fear of evil."*

Psalms 121:7, 8, *"The Lord shall preserve thee from all evil: He shall preserve thy soul. The Lord shall preserve thy going out and thy coming in from this time forth, and even for evermore."*

Ezekiel 34:28, *"And they shall no more be a prey to the heathen, neither shall the beast of the land devour them; but they shall dwell safely, and none shall make them afraid."*

Deuteronomy 33:12, *"...The beloved of the Lord shall dwell in safety by Him; and the Lord shall cover him all the day long, and he shall dwell between His shoulders."*

Hebrews 10:30, *"... Vengeance belongeth unto me, I will recompense, saith the Lord."*

Psalms 54:7, *"For He hath delivered me out of all trouble: and mine eye hath seen His desire upon mine enemies."*

<u>NOTES</u>

Chapter Thirteen
Travel Protection
Prayer

I address, rebuke, and bind you, Satan, and every evil spirit and power you rule, including the prince of the air, and cast all of you into outer darkness, in Jesus' name.

I bind and cast into the sea every evil assignment from Satan, and every evil source; all assignments of death, stroke, sickness, accidents, harm and injury, mechanical failures, tire failures, weakness, tiredness, sleepiness, un- alertness on my part, or any driver I pass, both coming, and going. I say to every evil assignment against us, "Be thou removed, and be thou cast into the sea," in Jesus' name, and according to **Mark 11:23.** Thus saith the Lord, *" For Verily I say unto you, that whosoever shall say unto this mountain, Be thou removed, and be thou cast into the sea; and shall not doubt in his heart, but shall believe that those things which he saith shall come to pass; he shall have whatsoever he saith."* **Mark 11:24**, *"Therefore I say unto you, What things soever ye desire, when ye pray, believe that ye receive them, and ye shall have them."*

II Timothy 1:7, *"For God hath not given us the spirit of fear; but of power, and of love, and of a sound mind."* I thank you Father, that as I travel, you deliver me from every type of evil, and preserve me for your Kingdom; therefore, I am at peace, because I travel in safety. **Psalms 91:4, 9-12, *"He shall cover thee with his feathers, and under His wings shalt thou trust: His truth shall be thy shield and buckler." "Because thou hast made the Lord, which is my refuge, even the Most High, thy habitation; There shall no evil befall thee, neither shall any plague come nigh thy dwelling. For He shall give His angels charge over thee, to keep thee in all thy ways. They shall bear thee up in their hands, lest thou dash thy foot against a stone."***

I declare, that all traffic around me moves smoothly at all times, and I will not be subjected to delays, or stops.

I Loose the Anointing of God over my passengers, my vehicle, and myself. I plead the Blood of Jesus over us and declare, that we travel in complete safety, and we arrive refreshed and invigorated. I declare that the angels of the Lord are dispatched over us, to make sure of our total protection, lest we dash our foot against a stone. *"...be it unto me according to thy Word*," **Luke 1:38,** in Jesus' name, Amen.

NOTES

Travel Protection Scriptures

Luke 21:18, *"But there shall not an hair of your head perish."*

Luke 10:19, *"Behold, I give unto you power to tread on serpents and scorpions, and over all the power of the enemy: and nothing shall by any means hurt you."*

Isaiah 55:11,12, *"So shall my word be that goeth forth out of my mouth: it shall not return unto me void, but it shall accomplish that which I please, and it shall prosper in the thing whereto I sent it. For ye shall go out with joy, and be led forth with peace: the mountains and the hills shall break forth before you into singing, and all the trees of the field shall clap their hands."*

II Timothy 4:18, *"And the Lord shall deliver me from every evil work, and will preserve me unto His heavenly Kingdom: to whom be glory for ever and ever. Amen."*

Proverbs 18:10, *"The name of the Lord is a strong tower: the righteous runneth into it, and is safe."*

John 14:14, *"If ye shall ask anything in my name, I will do it."*

Psalms 3:3, *"But thou, O Lord, art a shield for me; my glory, and the lifter up of mine head."*

Proverbs 29:25, *"The fear of man bringeth a snare: but whoso putteth his trust in the Lord shall be safe."*

Job 10:12, *"Thou hast granted me life and favour, and thy visitation hath preserved my spirit."*

You will find many more scriptures to stand on for travel protection under the Chapter, "Protection Prayer and Scriptures."

<u>NOTES</u>

Chapter Fourteen
Prayer of Dedication

I bind Satan and all demonic dominion, from stealing the Word, and all of these benefits from my spouse, children, pastors, our family members, and myself. I cast into the sea, all assignments of evil from every source, against each of us, in Jesus' name.

My Dear Heavenly Father, I come into your gates with Thanksgiving, and into your courts with praise by the Blood of Jesus, and I seek first the Kingdom of God, and your Righteousness. I Loose the Anointing of God over me, to attend and keep thy Words, laws, and commandments. Lead and guide me, let me not be deceived, and teach my tongue to use knowledge aright. I declare that I am a counselor of peace and might, that I have joy, a merry heart, a cheerful countenance, a soft answer to turn away wrath, and a wholesome tongue. God gives me wisdom, instruction, understanding, knowledge, discernment, discretion, justice, judgment, integrity, equity, mercy, grace, truth, honor, and riches.

I declare my complete covenant rights, divine health, total prosperity in all things, and joy, by the words of my mouth. I declare that I am a good steward of my wealth. I commit my works unto you Lord Jesus; ask that you establish my thoughts, direct my steps daily, and let me stand perfect, and complete, and express all of God's will. I loose the Anointing of God over me for a good name, extreme favor, humility, and a fear of the Lord. I loose the Anointing of God over me for total wisdom and understanding of all the benefits which you have provided us, through your Name, your Blood, your Power, your Spirit, your Authority, and your Word; and how we use each, for our maximum benefit.

Colossians 3:16, *"Let the Word of Christ dwell in you richly in all wisdom."*

I loose the Anointing of God over me, for the manifestation of the Spirit to impart unto me, according to **I Corinthians 12:7-10**. To impart to me the Word of wisdom, the Word of knowledge, faith, the gifts of healing, the working of miracles, prophesy, discerning of spirits, divers tongues, and interpretation; dividing unto me severally as He will, that I may profit with all. I commit my works unto you, Lord; and Loose the Anointing of God over me, to establish my thoughts, to prepare my heart, and the answers of my tongue, that I may please you. I loose the Anointing, and the ability of God, to show me the purpose for my life, and the definite plans for success, and prosperity in all things.

I loose the power in all of these scriptures over me, from the top of my head, to the soles of my feet. I receive the manifestation of all of these benefits and covenant promises in the name of Jesus Christ. **Luke 1:37,38,** *"For with God nothing shall be impossible"* *"... be it unto me according to thy Word,"* *in Jesus' name, AMEN!*

NOTES

Scriptures

Mark 4:14, *"The sower soweth the Word."*

Isaiah 55:11, *"So shall my Word be that goeth forth out of my mouth: it shall not return unto me void, but it shall accomplish that which I please, and it shall prosper in the thing whereto I sent it."*

Proverbs 1:23, *"Turn you at my reproof: behold, I will pour out my spirit unto you, I will make known my Words unto you."*

Isaiah 59:21, *"As for me, this is my covenant with them, saith the Lord; My Spirit...and my Words... shall not depart out of thy mouth forever."*

Psalms 68:19, *"Blessed be the Lord, who daily loadeth us with benefits, even the God of our salvation."*

Luke 21:33, *"Heaven and Earth shall pass away: but my Words shall not pass away."*

Psalms 18:30, *"As for God, His way is perfect: the Word of the Lord is tried: He is a buckler to all those that trust in Him."*

Psalms 20:5, ***"We will rejoice in thy salvation, and in the name of our God we will set up our banners: The Lord fulfill all thy petitions."***

II Corinthians 1:20, *"For all the promises of God in Him (Jesus) are yea, and in Him Amen, unto the glory of God by us."*

Psalms 46:1,7, *"God is our refuge and strength, a very present help in trouble." "The Lord of Hosts is with us; the God of Jacob is our refuge." Selah*

Isaiah 40:29,31, *"He giveth power to the faint: and to them that have no might He increaseth strength." "But they that wait upon the Lord shall renew their strength; they shall mount up with wings as eagles; they shall run, and not be weary; and they shall walk and not faint."*

THE PRAYER OF JABEZ, *I Chronicles 4:10,* *"... Oh that thou wouldest bless me indeed, and enlarge my coast, and that thine hand might be with me, and that thou wouldest keep me from evil, that it may not grieve me!"*

<u>Notes</u>

Chapter Fifteen
Prosperity Prayer

Ephesians 6:10 Tells me to be, **"... strong in the Lord, and in the power of His might."** I wear the whole Armor of God, of **Ephesians 6:11-18.** Under the protection of the Blood of Jesus Christ which I apply to me, and with the authority vested in me by Christ Himself, I now bind, and loose according to **Matthew 18:18.** I bind and cast into outer darkness Satan, all principalities, powers, borders, rulers, thrones, gates, the prince of the air, and all evil spirits. I bind them all away from my finances, properties, business, possessions, my family, myself and cast them into outer darkness. I bind all evil assignments, and I say, be thou removed, and be thou cast into the sea; along with every cause and effect against me and my family, our finances, possessions, properties, and businesses, both currently, and in the future, in the name, and in the Blood of Jesus Christ.

I Corinthians 2:9, *"...Eye hath not seen, nor ear heard, neither have entered into the heart of man, the things which God hath prepared for them that love him."*

I make this decree and declaration unto God for Supernatural wealth, all of God's covenant promises, and summons it all to me now, in Jesus' name! I ask for the power to get wealth, which will propel me into a major end-time harvest giver. I ask for the ability to give millions to help establish the covenant that you swore to our forefathers as it is unto this day. I lay claim by demanding, calling forth, and commanding all the good that God has provided for me to come to me now, in Jesus' name!

I loose the ability and the Anointing of God over me, for revelation wisdom, and knowledge to speak God's Words, God's blessings, and His Covenant promises for financial prosperity, and riches for my life. I loose God's anointing over me for Supernatural power to get wealth: empowerment through dreams, visions, ideas, wisdom and inventions. I declare, and decree, the fulfillment of all the Abrahamic Covenant promises for my life. I loose all the good that God has prepared for me, to come to me now. I loose the maximum payback, for all that the enemy has stolen from my spouse and I, and our children. I loose the maximum return, for all that we have given.

I loose unto me, and mine, the un-reaped positive harvest of our physical and spiritual ancestors. I declare that I live under an open heaven, and have the extreme favor of God, and man, over my life. I decree an exponential multiplication of all my good seed sown, and total crop failure, of any bad seed sown.

According to **John 15:7**, "*If, ye abide in me, and My Words abide in you, ye shall ask what ye will, and It shall be done unto you.*" **I John 5:14** says, If we ask anything according to His will, and have confidence that God has to perform it, He will. So Lord, I have confidence and trust in you, and your Word, and according to **Mark 11:22-24,** I can have whatsoever I say, if I believe and doubt not. I ask for mighty, great, divine, abundant wealth. This money will be spent to help establish your covenant, and for my family, friends, the end-time harvest, and myself; for your glory, Lord.

I thank you God, that when I pray your Word, I am praying your will. **Jeremiah 1:12** says, that you will hasten (be active and alert over) your Word to perform it.

Genesis 4:10 declares, that the blood is a witness, and **Hebrews 12:24** tells us, that the blood speaks. I ask the blood of Jesus, to speak in my behalf concerning these blessings, because **Colossians 1:13** tells me, that Jesus bought them for me on the cross. God "Hath made us meet to be partakers of the inheritance of the saints in light:" **Colossians 1:12.**

Psalms 103:20, 21, *"Bless the Lord, ye His angels, that excel in strength, that do His commandments, hearkening unto the voice of His Word. Bless ye the Lord all ye His hosts; ye ministers of His, that do His pleasure."*

Joel 2:11, *"And the Lord shall utter His voice before His army: for His camp is very great; for He is strong that executeth His Word:"*

Hebrews 1:14, *"Are they not all ministering spirits, sent forth to minister for them who shall be heirs of salvation?"*

I declare, and thank you Lord, that your angels establish our Words, which are based on your Words, here on earth, and, cause our good to come to us. I NOW LOOSE THE ANOINTING OF GOD FOR A BREAKTHROUGH FOR MONEY, AND FOR A BREAKTHROUGH OF ALL MY COVENANT PROMISES.

I CLAIM, AND LOOSE MY HARVEST TO COME TO ME! I LOOSE THE POWER IN ALL OF THESE SCRIPTURES, AND THE ANOINTING OF GOD, FOR BREAKTHROUGH FOR THIS GREAT WEALTH AND PROSPERITY TO SUDDENLY BE RELEASED UPON ME. I STAND ON THE WORD OF GOD FOR THIS DECREE TO BE MADE MANIFEST. I RECEIVE AND BIND ALL OF THESE COVENANT BLESSINGS TO ME NOW.

Luke 1:37, 38, *"For with God nothing shall be impossible." "...Be it unto me, according to thy Word."* It is established in Jesus' name! Amen and Amen!

_____
                          Signature   Date

Prosperity Teachings

DESIRE, DECISION, FAITH, PERSISTENCE, AND ORGANIZED PLANNING ARE THE MASTER-MIND GROUP.
THOUGHT BACKED BY DESIRE HAS A TENDENCY TO CHANGE ITSELF INTO ITS PHYSICAL EQUIVALENT.

Four benefits to obtain wealth:

1. A definite purpose backed by burning desire for its fulfillment.

2. A definite plan, expressed in continuous action.

3. A mind closed tightly against all negative and discouraging influences.

4. Two or more agreeing together and encouraging each other to follow through.

SECRETS OF FAITH BUILDING

Continually say what God said, and meditate on the Word! God's Word is Truth, and it is faith filled.

"But my God shall supply all your need according to His riches in glory by Christ Jesus." **Philippians 4:19.**

Determine that you will train your spirit, and your mind, with the Word of God. Say, <u>I choose to believe what the Word says about me</u>. Faith brings God on the scene. If it doesn't agree with the Word of God, don't believe it, and don't do it!

Five Points of Prosperity
By Pastor Jeff Hackleman

1. Ask God for wisdom daily.
2. Get a plan and be faithful to it. Learn to involve God in tithing 10% of everything.
3. Save 10% for yourself. Live off the top of the barrel - not the bottom.
4. Keep a healthy attitude about your job.

Colossians 3:23,24, *"And whatsoever ye do, do it heartily, as to the Lord, and not unto men; Knowing that of the Lord ye shall receive the reward of the inheritance: for ye serve the Lord Christ."*

5. Speak words of faith over your financial condition. Declare God's Words over your finances and your business.

I John 3:22, *"And whatsoever we ask, we receive of Him, because we keep His commandments, and do those things that are pleasing in His sight."*

PROSPERITY SCRIPTURES

II Corinthians 2:14, *"Now thanks be unto God, which always causeth us to triumph in Christ..."*

John 14:13,14, *"And whatsoever ye shall ask in my name, that will I do" "...If ye shall ask anything in my name, I will do it."*

Proverbs 8:21, *"That I may cause those that love me to inherit substance; and I will fill their treasures."*

Psalms 89:34, God said, *"My covenant will I not break, nor alter the thing that is gone forth out of my lips."*

Psalms 65:11,"Thou crownest the year with thy goodness; and thy paths drop fatness." (Thy bounty*)*

Psalms 71:21, *"Thou shalt increase my greatness, and comfort me on every side."*

Proverbs 15:6, *"In the house of the righteous is much treasure; but in the revenues of the wicked is trouble."*

Proverbs 22:4, *"By humility and the fear of the Lord are riches, and honor, and life."*

Genesis 8:22, *"While the earth remaineth seedtime and harvest, and cold and heat, and summer and winter, and day and night shall not cease."*

II Corinthians 9:10, II, *"Now He that ministereth seed to the sower both minister bread for your food, and multiply your seed sown, and increase the fruits of your righteousness; Being enriched in everything to all bountifulness, which causeth through us thanksgiving to God:"*

II Corinthians 8:9, *"For ye know the grace of our Lord Jesus Christ, that, though He was rich, yet for your sakes He became poor, that ye through His poverty might be rich."*

Proverbs 22:29, *"Seest thou a man diligent in his business? he shall stand before kings; he shall not stand before mean men."*

Isaiah 45:2, 3, *"I will go before thee, and make the crooked places straight: I will break in pieces the gates of brass, and cut in sunder the bars of iron: And I will give thee the treasures of darkness, and hidden riches of secret places, that thou mayest know that I, the Lord, which call thee by thy name, am the God of Israel."*

Joel 2:25, 26, *"And I will restore to you, the years that the* locust hath eaten, the cankerworm, and the caterpillar, and the palmerworm, my great army which I sent among you." (The years spent in sin) " And ye shall eat in plenty, and be satisfied, and praise the name of the Lord your God, that hath dealt wondrously with you: and my people shall never be ashamed."

Deuteronomy 7:9, "Know therefore that the Lord thy God, He is God, the faithful God, which keepeth covenant and mercy with them that love Him, and keep His commandments to a thousand generations."

Psalms 94:14, "For the Lord will not cast off His people, neither will He forsake his inheritance."

Psalms 35:27, "Let them shout for joy and be glad, that favor my righteous cause: yea, let them say continually, Let the Lord be Magnified, which hath pleasure in the prosperity of His servant."

Deuteronomy 8:18, "But thou shalt remember the Lord thy God: For it is He that giveth thee power to get wealth, that He may establish His covenant which He sware unto thy fathers, as it is this day."

Psalms 68:19, "Blessed be the Lord, who daily loadeth us with benefits, even the God of our salvation."

Job 23:28, 24, 25, "Thou shalt also decree a thing, and it shall be established unto thee: and the light shall shine upon thy ways." "Then shalt thou lay up gold as dust, and the gold of O'phir as the stones of the brooks. Yea, the Almighty shall be thy defense, and thou shalt have plenty of silver."

Psalms 105:24 " And He increased His people greatly, and made them stronger than their enemies."

Proverbs 13:22 "…The wealth of the sinner is laid up for the just."

Proverbs 10:22 "The blessing of the Lord, it maketh rich, and He addeth no sorrow with It."

Deuteronomy 28:2-13, If we keep your commandments oh Lord, you will set us on high above all nations of the earth: "And all these blessings shall come on thee, and overtake thee, Blessed shalt thou be in the city, and blessed shalt thou be in the field, Blessed shall be the fruit of thy body, and the fruit of thy ground, and the fruit of thy cattle, the increase of thy kine, and the flocks of thy sheep. Blessed shall be thy basket and thy store. Blessed shalt thou be when thou comest in, and blessed shalt thou be when thou *goest out. The Lord shall cause thine enemies that rise up against thee to be smitten before thy face: they shall come out against thee one way, and flee before thee seven ways.* **The Lord shall command the blessing upon thee in thy storehouses, and in all that thy settest thine hand unto; and He shall bless thee in the land which the Lord thy God giveth thee.** *The Lord shall establish thee an Holy people unto himself, as He hath sworn unto thee, if thou shalt keep the commandments of the Lord thy God, and walk in His ways."* *"...And all people of the earth shall see that thou art called by the name of the Lord; and they shall be afraid of thee. And the Lord shall make thee plenteous in goods, in the fruit of thy body, thy cattle, and in the fruit of thy ground, in the land which the Lord sware unto thy fathers to give thee.* **The Lord shall open unto thee His good treasure, the heaven to give the rain unto thy land in His season, and to bless all the work of thine hand**; *and thou shalt lend unto many nations, and thou shalt not borrow.* **And the Lord shall make thee the head, and not the tail; and thou shalt be above only, and thou shalt not be beneath**; *if that thou hearken unto the commandments of the Lord thy God, which I command thee this day, to observe and to do them."*

Psalms 112:1- 3, "...Blessed is the man that feareth the Lord, that delighteth greatly in His commandments. His seed shall be mighty upon earth: the generation of the upright shall be blessed. Wealth and riches shall be in his house, and his righteousness endureth forever."

Hebrews 13:5, "...for He hath said, I will never leave thee, nor forsake thee."

Philippians 4:19, "*But my God shall supply all your need according to His riches in glory by Christ Jesus."*

Isaiah 58:11, "And the Lord shall guide thee continually, and satisfy thy soul in drought, and make fat thy bones: and thou shalt be like a watered garden, and like a spring of water, whose waters fail not."

Exodus 33:19, And He said, *"I will make all my goodness pass before thee, and I will proclaim the name of the Lord before thee; and will be gracious to whom I will be gracious, and will shew mercy on whom I will shew mercy."*

Galations 6:9, *"And let us not be weary in well doing: for in due season we shall reap, if we faint not."*

Psalms 13:6, *"I will sing unto the Lord, because He hath dealt bountifully with me."*

Ecclesiastes *10:1,* *"A feast is made for laughter, and wine maketh merry:* **but money answereth all things."**

Proverbs 8:18, 19, *"Riches and honour are with me; yea, durable riches and righteousness. My fruit is better than gold, yea, than fine gold; and my revenue than choice silver."*

Job 22:28, *"Thou shalt also decree a thing, and it shall be established unto thee: and the light shall shine upon thy ways."*

Genesis 28:13-15, (Jacob's dream, God changed Jacobs name to Israel.) *"…I am the Lord God of Abraham thy Father, and the God of Isaac: The land whereon thou liest, to thee will I give it, and to thy seed: And thy seed shall be as the dust of the earth, and thou shalt spread abroad to the west, and to the east, and to the north, and to the south: and in thee and in thy seed shall all the families of the earth be blessed. And, behold, I am with thee, and will keep thee in all places whither thou goest, and will bring thee again into this land: for I will not leave thee, until I have done that which I have spoken to thee of."*

Proverbs 3:9,10, "Honour the Lord with thy substance, and with the firstfruits of all thine increase: so shall thy barns be filled with plenty, and thy presses shall burst out with new wine."

Deuteronomy 30:9, *"And the Lord thy God will make thee plenteous in every work of thine hand, in the fruit of thy body, and in the fruit of thy cattle, and in the fruit of thy land, for good: For the Lord will again rejoice over thee for good, as He rejoiced over thy fathers"*

Matthew 12:35, Jesus said, ***"A good man out of the good treasures of the heart bringeth forth good things:*** *and an evil man out of the evil treasure bringeth forth evil things:"* (Notice here that man, not God bringeth them forth. Again, we bring forth our good by what we speak out of our mouths.)

Ecclesiastes 5:18,19, *"Behold that which I have seen: it is good and comely for one to eat and to drink, and to enjoy the good of all his labour that he taketh under the sun all the days of his life,* which God giveth him: for it is his portion. **Every man also to whom God hath given riches and wealth, and hath given him power to eat thereof, and to take his portion, and to rejoice in his labour: this is the gift of God."**

Isaiah 30:23, *"Then shall He give the rain of thy seed, that thou shalt sow the ground withal: and bread of the increase of the earth, and it shall be fat and plenteous: in that day shall thy cattle feed in large pastures."*

Isaiah 48:17, *"Thus saith the Lord, thy Redeemer, the Holy One of Israel; I am the Lord thy God which teacheth thee to profit (prosper), which leadeth thee by the way that thou shouldest go."*

Ecclesiastes 3:13, *"And also that every man should eat and drink, and enjoy the good of all his labour, it is the gift of God."*

Deuteronomy 11:15, *"And I will send grass in thy fields for thy cattle, that thou mayest eat and be full."*

Psalms 128:2, *"For thou shalt eat the labour of thine hands: happy shalt thou be, and it shall be well with thee."*

Isaiah 65:21-23, *"And they shall build houses, and inhabit them; and they shall plant vineyards, and eat the fruit of them. They shall not build, and another inhabit; They shall not plant, and another eat: For as the days of a tree are the days of my people, and mine elect shall long enjoy the work of their hands. They shall not labour in vain, nor bring forth for trouble; for they are the seed of the blessed of the Lord, and their offspring with them."*

Psalms 1:3, **"And he shall be like a tree planted by the rivers of water, that bringeth forth his fruit in his season; his leaf also shall not wither; And whatsoever he doeth shall prosper."**

Genesis 12:1- 3, *"Now the Lord had said unto Abram, Get thee out of thy country, and from thy kindred, and from thy father's house, unto a land that I will shew thee: And I will make of thee a great nation, and I will bless thee, and make thy name great: And thou shalt be a blessing: And I will bless them that bless thee, and curse him that curseth thee; and in thee shall all families of the earth be blessed."*

Romans 8:32, "He that spared not His own son, but delivered Him up for us all, how shall He not with Him also freely give us all things?"

Luke 6:38, *"Give, and it shall be given unto you; good* *measure, pressed down, and shaken together, and running over, shall men give into your bosom. For with the same measure that ye mete withal it shall be measured to you again."*

Colossians 3:23,24, *"And whatsoever ye do, do it heartily, as to the Lord, and not unto men; knowing that of the Lord ye shall receive the reward of the inheritance: For ye serve the Lord, Christ."*

Matthew 7:7, 8, *"Ask, and it shall be given you; seek, and ye shall find; knock, and it shall be opened unto you: For every one that asketh receiveth; and he that seeketh findeth; and to him that knocketh it shall be opened."*

Matthew 21:22, *"And all things, whatsoever ye shall ask in prayer, believing, ye shall receive."*

Isaiah 30:19, *".... He will be very gracious unto thee at the voice of thy cry; when He shall hear it, He will answer thee."*

John 3:22, *"And whatsoever we ask, we receive of Him, because we keep His commandments, and do those things that are pleasing in His sight."*

Jeremiah 33:3, *"Call unto me, and I will answer thee, and shew thee great and mighty things, which thou knowest not."*

Mark 11:24, *"Therefore I say unto you, what things soever ye desire, when ye pray, believe that ye receive them, and ye shall have them."*

Deuteronomy 6:3, *"Hear therefore, O Israel, and observe to do it; that it may be well with thee, and that ye may increase mightily, as the Lord God of thy fathers hath promised thee, in the land that floweth with milk and honey."*

Deuteronomy 7:12, *"Wherefore it shall come to pass, if ye hearken to these judgments, and keep, and do them, that the Lord thy God shall keep unto thee the covenant and the mercy which He sware unto thy fathers:"*

Deuteronomy 29:9, *"Keep therefore the Words of this covenant, and do them, that ye may prosper in all that ye do."*

Deuteronomy 5:29, *"O that there were such an heart in them that they would fear me, and keep all my commandments always, that it might be well with them, and with their children for ever!"*

Job 36:11, *"If they obey and serve Him, they shall spend their days in prosperity, and their years in pleasures."*

Deuteronomy 4:31 *"(For the Lord thy God is a merciful God;)*

He will not forsake thee, neither destroy thee, nor forget the covenant of thy fathers which He sware unto them."

Psalms 105:8, *"He hath remembered His covenant forever, the Word which He commanded to a thousand generations."*

Hebrews 10:23, *"Let us hold fast the profession of our faith without wavering; (for He is faithful that promised;)"*

Isaiah 25:1, *"O Lord, thou art my God; I will exalt thee, I will praise thy name; for thou hast done wonderful things; thy counsels of old are faithfulness and truth."*

Psalms 9:10,"*And they that know thy name will put their trust in thee: For thou, Lord, hast not forsaken them that seek thee."*

Psalms 119:89, 90, *"For ever, O Lord, Thy Word is settled in heaven. Thy faithfulness is unto all generations..."*

Psalms 118:25, "Save now, I beseech thee, O Lord, I beseech thee send now prosperity."

Psalms 25:13,14, "His soul shall dwell at ease; and his seed shall inherit the earth. The secret of the Lord is with them that fear Him; and He will shew them His covenant."

I Chronicles 29:12,13, *"Both riches and honour come of thee, and thou reignest over all; and in thine hand is power and might; and in thine hand it is to make great and to give strength unto all. Now therefore, our God, we thank thee, and praise thy glorious name."*

Psalms 115:14, "The Lord shall increase you more and more, you and your children."

Proverbs 19:23, "The fear of the Lord *tendeth to life; and he that hath it shall abide satisfied;* (in great prosperity), **and he shall not be visited with evil."**

Psalms 23:1,5, "The Lord is my shepherd, I shall not want. He maketh me to lie down in green pastures. He leadeth me beside the still waters. He restoreth my soul: He leadeth me in the paths of righteousness for His name's sake. Yea, though I walk through the valley of the shadow of death, I will fear no evil: for thou art with me; thy rod and thy staff they comfort me. Thou preparest a table before me in the presence of mine enemies: thou anointest my head with oil; My cup runneth over. Surely goodness and mercy shall follow me all the days of my life: and I will dwell in the house of the Lord for ever."

<u>NOTES</u>

Chapter Sixteen
Tithing Confession
Scriptures

I confess that I am redeemed by the blood of the Lamb. Jesus Christ is my Chief High Priest. I am a citizen of the Kingdom of Almighty God. I thank you, God, for hearing my plea and delivering me from the power and authority of darkness, and for bringing me into the Kingdom of your dear Son.

I bring the first fruits of my income to you, Jesus, and I worship Almighty God with them. In faith, I am standing on your Word, that you will pour out more blessings than I have room to receive, because I keep your commandments. I thank you, Father, for rebuking the devourer for my sake. I ask you now, Lord, to command the hundredfold blessing upon me that you've promised in **Mark 10:30**, *"But he shall receive an hundredfold now in this time."* (When we give for His sake, and for the gospel's sake).

I loose and bind unto me, the Anointing of Almighty God for all of the Covenant blessings to be manifested unto me according to thy Word, in Jesus' name. Heavenly Father, I ask that you perform your Word for me now, according to thy Kingdom laws, in Jesus' name. Amen!

Malachi 3:10,11, *"Bring ye all the tithes into the storehouse, that there may be meat in mine house, and prove me now herewith, saith the Lord of hosts, if I will not open you the windows of heaven, and pour you out a blessing, that there shall not be room enough to receive it. And I will rebuke the devourer for your sakes, and he shall not destroy the fruits of your ground; neither shall your vine cast her fruit before the time in the field, saith the Lord of hosts."*

Proverbs 3:9,10, *"Honor the Lord with thy substance, and with the first fruits of all thine increase: So shall thy barns be filled with plenty, and thy presses shall burst out with new wine."*

Hebrews 10:23, *"Let us hold fast the profession of our faith without wavering:"(for He is faithful that promised;)*

Matthew 18:19, "...*if two of you shall agree on earth as touching any thing that they shall ask, it shall be done for them of my Father which is in heaven. For where two or three are gathered together in my name, there am I in the midst of them.*"

Mark.11:23, "Whosoever shall say...and shall not doubt...but shall believe that those things which he saith shall come to pass; He shall have whatsoever he saith." Ephesians 6:8, "Knowing that whatsoever good thing any man doeth, the same shall he receive of the Lord, whether he be bond or free."

When one is obedient to God's laws on tithing, and keeps His Commandments, he has the right to claim and expect God's covenant laws of prosperity.

Leviticus 26:2-5,9,10, *"Ye shall keep my Sabbaths, and reverence my sanctuary: I am the Lord. If ye walk in my statutes, and keep my commandments, and do them: Then I will give you rain in due season, and the land shall yield her increase, and the trees of the field shall yield their fruit.* **And your threshing shall reach unto the vintage, and the vintage shall reach unto the sowing time: and ye shall eat your bread to the full, and dwell in your land safely." "For I will have respect unto you, and make you fruitful, and multiply you, and establish my covenant with you. And ye shall eat old store, and bring forth the old because of the new."**

II Corinthians 9:6,7, " But this I say, He which soweth sparingly shall reap also sparingly; and he which soweth bountifully shall reap also bountifully. Every man according as he purposeth in his heart, so let him give, not grudgingly, or of necessity: for God loveth a cheerful giver."

II Corinthians 9:8-11, "And God is able to make all grace abound toward you; that ye, always having all sufficiency in all things, may abound to every good work: *(As it is written, He hath dispersed abroad; he hath given to the poor: his righteousness remaineth for ever. Now He that ministereth seed to the sower both minister bread for your food, and multiply your seed sown, and increase the fruits of your righteousness;) Being enriched in every thing to all bountifulness, which causeth through us thanksgiving to God."*

Luke 6:38, *"Give, and it shall be given unto you; good*

measure, pressed down, and shaken together, and running over, shall men give unto your bosom. For with the same measure that ye mete withal it shall be measured to you again."

II Chronicles 24:20, *"And the spirit of God came upon Zechariah the son of Jehoiada the priest, which stood above the people, and said unto them, Thus saith God, Why transgress ye the commandments of the Lord, that ye cannot prosper? Because ye have forsaken the Lord, He hath also forsaken you."*

Psalms 22:25,26, *"My praise shall be of thee in the great congregation: I will pay my vows before them that fear him. The meek shall eat and be satisfied: they shall praise the Lord that seek him: your heart shall live for ever."*

Psalms 50:14, *"Offer unto God thanksgiving; and pay thy vows unto the most High:"*

Psalms 104:14-15, *"He causeth the grass to grow for the cattle, and herb for the service of man; that He may bring forth food out of the earth; And wine that maketh glad the heart of man, and oil to make his face to shine, and bread which strengtheneth man's heart."*

Isaiah 58:10,11, *"And if thou draw out thy soul to the hungry, and satisfy the afflicted soul; then shall thy light rise in obscurity, and thy darkness be as the noon day; And the Lord shall guide thee continually, and satisfy thy soul in drought, and make fat thy bones: and thou shalt be like a watered garden, and like a spring of water, whose waters fail not."*

Joel 2:23-26, *"Be glad then, ye children of Zion, and rejoice in the Lord your God: for He hath given you the former rain moderately, and He will cause to come down for you the rain, the former rain, and the latter rain in the first month. And the floors shall be full of wheat, and the vats shall overflow with wine and oil. And I will restore to you the years that the locust hath eaten, the cankerworm, and the caterpillar, and the palmerworm, My great army which I sent among you. And ye shall eat in plenty, and be satisfied, and praise the name of the Lord your God, that hath dealt wondrously with you: and my people shall never be ashamed."*

Psalms 23: *"The Lord is my shepherd, I shall not want. He maketh me to lie down in green pastures: He leadeth me beside* *the still waters. He restoreth my soul: He leadeth me in the paths of righteousness for His name's sake. Yea, though I walk through the valley of the shadow of death, I will fear no evil: for thou art with me; thy rod and thy staff they comfort me. Thou preparest a table before me in the presence of mine enemies: thou anointest my head with oil; **my cup runneth over**. Surely goodness and mercy shall follow me all the days of my life; and I will dwell in the house of the Lord forever."*

Psalms 1:1-3, *"Blessed is the man that walketh not in the counsel of the ungodly, nor standeth in the way of sinners, nor sitteth in the seat of the scornful. **But his delight is in the law of the Lord; and in His law doth he meditate day and night. And he shall be like a tree planted by the rivers of water, that bringeth forth his fruit in his season; his leaf also shall not wither; and whatsoever he doeth shall prosper.***"*

Isaiah 32:18, *"**And my people shall dwell in a peaceable habitation, and in sure dwellings, and in quiet resting places;**"*

Deuteronomy 8:10,11,18, *"When thou hast eaten and art full, then thou shalt bless the Lord thy God for the good land which He hath given thee. Beware that thou forget not the Lord thy God, in not keeping His commandments, and His judgments, and His statutes, which I command thee this day:" " **But thou shalt remember the Lord thy God: for it is He that giveth thee power to get wealth, that He may establish His covenant which He sware unto thy fathers, as it is this day.***"*

Romans 8:32, *"He that spared not His own son, but delivered Him up for us all, how shall He not with Him also freely give us all things?"*

John 15:7, *"**If ye abide in me, and my Words abide in you, ye shall ask what ye will, and it shall be done unto you:**"*
There are many more prosperity scriptures in the Prosperity Chapter.

Chapter Seventeen
Prophesying The Word

God used prophesying to bring forth Christ Jesus into this world. John the Baptist was the forerunner of Jesus. John prepared the way for Jesus to come with the Words that he prophesied. We are the prophesiers of our futures. We prophesy that which we want to bring forth into our lives, by speaking, by confessing, and by backing that which we speak, and desire, with the Word of God.

Jesus said in **Matthew 11:11,12,** *"Verily I say unto you, among them that are born of women there hath not risen a greater than John the Baptist: not with-standing he that is least in the Kingdom of heaven is greater than he. And from the days of John the Baptist until now the Kingdom of heaven suffereth violence, and the violent take it by force."* Jesus said, there was none greater than John the Baptist. He prepared the way for Jesus to come, he confessed it, he prophesied it, and Jesus came to fulfill John's confession and all prophecies. The least of us is greater than John, if we are citizens of the Kingdom of heaven. God is obligated to His Word; He is obligated to come into every situation that we confess, that we prophesy about. Jesus' ministry was to fulfill prophecy. We are also told in **Revelation 19:10,** "… *for the testimony of Jesus is the Spirit of prophecy."*

When we put God's Word into our mouths and speak it, declare it, decree it, confess it, and proclaim it over our lives and our situations, we are prophesying and we have the ear, of God Almighty. The same God that put the stars, the moon, and the whole universe into place, is the same God that watches over the Words we speak, to perform them. **Hebrews 1:3** tells us, that God is *"upholding all things by the Word of His power."* Therefore God's Word sustains the Universe, and He will see to it that we have what we say, when we back our words by standing on, and speaking, His Word. **II Timothy 3:16** tells us, "*all scripture is given by inspiration of God."*

It was Jesus' job to bring prophecies to pass when the prophets prophesied by the inspiration of God. He still today brings to pass what we say or prophesy, when we profess, and confess, the Word over our lives, and situations. Whether it be healing for our bodies, salvation for our lost loved ones, or financial riches, Jesus watches over His Words to perform them, to bring them to pass when we speak them.

We know that salvation of our souls and eternal life, is God's greatest gift to mankind. If we confess with our mouths and our words are in agreement with His Word, we shall be saved. Salvation, therefore, comes through prophecy. **Romans 10:8-10,** *"But what saith it? The Word is nigh thee, even in thy mouth, and in thy heart: that is, the Word of faith, which we preach: That if thou shalt confess with thy mouth the Lord Jesus, and shalt believe in thine heart that God hath raised Him from the dead, thou shalt be saved. For with the heart man believeth unto righteousness; and with the mouth confession is made unto salvation,"* (resulting in salvation). Not only do we prophesy our way unto salvation by having faith and believing in God, we also prophesy the other covenant gifts, like healing and wealth, through speaking, and standing on God's Word in faith.

This is the principle I stood on, along with many other healing scriptures, as I prayed over every bag of John's chemotherapy before it was administered to him. I declared that it would not make him sick, nauseated, weak; nor would it make him bald. It did not. The principle of prophesying, confessing that which one desires, and backing it up with the Word of God, is the way great miracles of healing, great financial breakthroughs, and various other wonderful gifts are manifested on a continual basis in our church, Family Faith Church, in Huntsville, Texas.

Back up your prophesies with God's Word. God has always used prophesying to bring all scripture into reality; therefore, it behooves us to back up our Words, with God's Word. I trust that you will pray along with me, speaking God's Words over your life and over your situations to frame your world; just like God used His Words, to frame His world. Praise God for sending Jesus, to show us how to do it.

This book is a "how to" course, a training manual, or seminar, if you will. It is ready, waiting at your fingertips, to take you into God's presence and lead you, showing you how to profess and decree God's Word, by example. Pray along with me. This is the way God created everything that was created – He spoke everything into existence*!*

In **Luke 8:11,15 ,** Jesus gave the parable of the sower. He tells us, *"Now the parable is this: The seed is the Word of God."* And then He tells us, *"But that on the good ground are they, which in an honest and good heart, having heard the Word,* (it has to be spoken in order to hear it), *keep it, and bring forth fruit with patience."* This verse also tells us that <u>we bring forth fruit (whatever we desire), by speaking the Word, hearing the Word, and keeping the Word. We keep it before our eyes, speak it with our mouths, prophesying it, and keeping it in our hearts.</u>

In the first chapter of **Genesis,** God showed us how He did it, how He called everything into being. In **Genesis 1:2,** *"…. And the Spirit of God moved upon the face of the waters."* This is the way God is telling us, that God's Spirit is hovering and brooding, over those things we call forth. God's Spirit is ready to give birth to the desires of your heart. God's Spirit is waiting to bring forth your healing, your prosperity, all of your covenant promises, such as your next job, business, or whatever you desire.

In **Ezekiel 37:4,** God carried Ezekiel out in the Spirit of the Lord and set him down in a valley of dry bones and said unto him, *"…Prophesy upon these bones, and say unto them, O ye dry bones, hear the Word of the Lord."* Read the entire chapter of **Ezekiel 37,** to see how He did it. In **verses 7-10,** Ezekiel said, *"So I prophesied as I was commanded: and as I prophesied there was a noise, and behold a shaking, and the bones came together, bone to his bone. And when I beheld, lo, the sinews and the flesh came up upon them, and the skin covered them above: but there was no breath in them. Then said He unto me, prophesy unto the wind, prophesy, son of man, and say to the wind, thus saith the Lord God; Come from the four winds, O breath, and breathe upon these slain, that they may live. So I prophesied as He commanded me, and the breath came into them, and they lived, and stood up upon their feet, an exceeding great army."*

<u>**Something similar happened the day John came back to life.**</u> After binding and casting into outer darkness all evil including the prince of the air and the spirit of death and stroke; <u>**my son, and I prophesied over John, on going, without stopping, until he**</u>

came back to life.

I used John's name in the scriptures instead of I. I declared **Psalms 118:17** over him, **John, "...shall not die, but live, and declare the works of the Lord." And, "For the law of the Spirit of life in Christ Jesus hath made (John) free from the law of sin and death.**" *Romans 8:2.* I continued, declaring more of God's Word over John, **Isaiah 53:4,5,** *and* **I Peter 2:24**, which tells us that we are healed by the stripes of Jesus. Also, I pled the Blood of Jesus over John. **After we prayed twenty to thirty minutes, the breath came back into him and he lived, and stood up upon his feet, for about another three months**!

The apostle Paul in *Ephesians 6:11* challenges us to, *"Put on the whole armor of God, that ye may be able to stand against the wiles of the devil."* We are in actual battle daily, with the prince of this world over our Kingdom rights and privileges. Verse **12** explains, *"For we wrestle not against flesh and blood, but against principalities, against powers, against the rulers of the darkness of this world, against spiritual wickedness in high places."* Our enemy the devil, has come to kill, to steal, and to destroy; but we can win. We can be successful, prosperous, healthy and whole.... it is our covenant right.

In **Jeremiah 1:8-10** we learn, *"Be not afraid of their faces: **for I am with thee to deliver thee, saith the Lord**. Then the Lord put forth his hand and touched my mouth, and the Lord said unto me, **Behold, I have put my Words in thy mouth. See, I have this day set thee over the nations and over the kingdoms, to root out, and to pull down, and to destroy, and to throw down, to build, and to plant**."*

Isn't this exciting? God has given us everything we need to be winners! He has told us to put on the whole armor of God and He has given us His Words to put in our mouths to defeat Satan and all of our foes with. Our most awesome primary weapons, the Word of God, the Name and the Blood of Jesus, allows us to defeat Satan, and every enemy, every time.

Who might you ask, is this church of Jesus Christ? We are the church of Jesus Christ. We are His body and we represent Him on the earth today. Let us arise and be in unity with the other members of the body of Christ. **I Corinthians 12:12-14, 20,** *"For as the body is one, and hath many members, and all the members* *of that one body, being many, are one body: so also is Christ. For by one Spirit are we all baptized into one body, whether we be Jews or Gentiles, whether we be bond or free; and have been all made to drink into one Spirit. For the body is not one member, but many." "But now are they many members, yet but one body."* And in **Romans 12:4,5,** we are told, *"For as we have many members in one body, and all members have not the same office: So we, being many, are one body in Christ, and every one members one of another."* And in **John 17: 11,18,20-23,** we find Jesus praying unto God, *"...Holy Father, keep through thine own name those whom thou hast given me, that they may be one, as we are."*

" As thou hast sent me into the world, even so have I also sent them into the world." "Neither pray I for these alone, but for them also which shall believe on me through their word: That they all may be one; as thou, Father, art in me, and I in thee, that they also may be one in us: that the world may believe that thou hast sent me. And the glory which thou gavest me I have given them; that they may be one, even as we are one: I in them, and thou in me, that they may be made perfect in one; and that the world may know that thou hast sent me, and hast loved them, as thou hast loved me." Everyone who is saved is the church of the living God. **Romans 10:9,10** tells us who is saved; *"That if thou shalt confess with thy mouth the Lord Jesus, and shalt believe in thine heart that God hath raised Him from the dead, thou shalt be saved. For with the heart man believeth unto righteousness; and with the mouth confession is made unto salvation."*

Nowhere in the Bible can I find reference to any denomination. I cannot find named the Methodist Church, the Baptist Church, the Pentecostal Church, the Assembly of God Church, the Presbyterian Church, the Nazarene, the Catholic, nor any other religion. The Bible tells us what we have to do to be saved, and, that we are all the many members of one body, which makes up the whole body of Christ. We are the Church of God. Therefore, we are all brothers and sisters in the Lord.

When we, the church of the living God, join forces and march together as one body, we will make a very threatening presence to our enemy, and have awesome conquering ability. We are a mighty, powerful force; we are an exceeding great army. It is time that we, who make up the army of the living God, stand with our armor in place; and take up our sword and shield; and start taking dominion over that which He has given us. He has given us dominion over the earth and all things in it, whatsoever we desire. We take dominion by prophesying and by taking it (our covenant promises), by force. To be an overcomer, we have to deal with the enemy, the accuser of the brethren, the devil, we have to over come him. <u>Child of the Lord, draw your sword, the awesome Word of God. Take up the mighty name of Jesus, stand up and fight.</u>

We are on a battlefield, the battlefield of the Lord. It is our calling as Christians to be warriors for God. <u>Stand up and fight – fight the good fight of faith. Prophesy, put God's Word in your heart and speak it with your mouth, and fight! The devil, our adversary, is afraid of us. He is afraid of "The Word,"(God) when we speak it with our mouths. He knows that the Word defeats him when we speak it, so does the precious name, and Blood of Jesus</u>. The Word is our foundation, we believe, and then we speak! **II Corinthians 4:13,14,** *"We having the same spirit of faith, according as it is written, I believed, and therefore have I spoken; we also believe, and therefore speak; Knowing that He which raised up the Lord Jesus shall raise us up also by Jesus,"* Let us Say, Say, Say, let us speak the Word!

<u>If we do not open our mouths and speak, proclaiming God's Word and God's promises – we lose! Whether we win or whether we lose, is up to us</u>! Life or death, wealth or poverty, health or sickness, is all determined by whether or not we speak the Word with our mouths and proclaim God's promises over our lives. Prophesy child of God. We can change what needs changing in our lives and rearrange that which needs rearranging in our lives, with Prayer in Jesus' name, and with the living Word of God.

Proverbs 6:2, *"Thou art snared with the words of thy mouth, thou art taken with the words of thy mouth."* Jesus took dominion and we are to take dominion, over our lives, and over our environment. Jesus spoke to the water and to the wind. Jesus spoke to demons, He even spoke to trees. He cursed the fig tree at the roots and told it that no man would eat fruit from it, forever. <u>Jesus spoke His Fathers Words with authority and they created things. We also are to speak our Father's Words, with authority, to</u>

create things. Jesus also never spoke words of negativity, neither should you or I.

To proclaim, or to make a proclamation or confession to God, means to say the same thing as God, to say what God has already said. That isn't too hard! Jesus intercedes for us when we are obedient and do as He did, when we speak as He spoke. He then takes the next step for us. I find it most awesome and most gratifying to know that the King of Kings, and the Lord of Lords, is interceding for us before the Father. Jesus is our High Priest. Isn't that overwhelming? Following is a few scriptures to confirm that.

Hebrews 3:1 shows Jesus as "The High Priest" of our profession, so let us make the right confessions. Let us say what He has said and He will intercede for us. *"Wherefore, holy brethren, partakers of the heavenly calling, consider the Apostle and High Priest of our profession, Christ Jesus;"*

Hebrews 4:14, *"Seeing then that we have a great high priest, that is passed into the heavens, Jesus the son of God, let us hold fast our profession."* **Hebrews 4:15,** *"For we have not an high priest which cannot be touched with the feeling of our infirmities; but was in all points tempted like as we are, yet without sin."* **Hebrews 4:16,** *"Let us therefore come boldly unto the throne of grace, that we may obtain mercy, and find grace to help in time of need."* **Hebrews 10:21-23,** *"And having an high priest over the house of God, Let us draw near with a true heart in full assurance of faith, (for He is faithful that promised)."*

Psalms 20:5, *"We will rejoice in thy salvation, and in the name of our God we will set up our banners: the Lord fulfill all thy petitions."*

Let us not give the devil a chance by opening our mouths and speaking negatively. Instead, profess, "Jesus is my Chief High Priest. God will not fail me". It is the forces of hell that try to make us speak negatively about our situations and to make our professions failures.

The Word of God is our prophesied destiny. Let us learn the Word, it is the blueprint for our future. Our words are self-fulfilling prophecies -whether positive or negative. Let us use God's blueprint TO BUILD OUR FUTURES!

<u>NOTES</u>

Chapter Eighteen

Be a Winner
A Prayer for Winners

To be the winner in life that God created us to be, we have to follow in the footsteps of Jesus and do as He did. **Philippians 4:9, "Those things, which ye have both learned, and received, and heard, and seen in me, do: and the God of peace shall be with you."**

In **Isaiah 41:15,16,** *"Behold, I will make thee a new sharp threshing instrument having teeth: thou shalt thresh the mountains, and beat them small, and shalt make the hills as chaff. Thou shalt fan them, and the wind shall carry them away, and the whirlwind shall scatter them: and thou shalt rejoice in the Lord, and shalt glory in the Holy One of Israel."* We thresh, beat and make our mountains, our problems, as chaff, so the wind shall scatter them, by opening our mouths and claiming, by speaking the Word of God over our problems, whatever they may be.

The Word of God is our sword; we are using it by professing and confessing it over our problems. When we back our prayers with the Word of God, it makes us like a new sharp instrument having teeth. **Isaiah 49:2, "...He hath made my mouth like a sharp sword;"**

We advance God's Kingdom by proclamation. **Isaiah 41:21,22,** "Produce your cause, saith the Lord; bring forth your strong reasons, saith the King of Jacob. Let them bring them forth, and shew us what shall happen: let them shew the former things, what they be, that we may consider them and know the latter end of them; **or declare for us things to come." Isaiah 42:9, "Behold, the former things are come to pass and new things do I declare: before they spring forth I tell you of them."** We are told in **Isaiah 43:26, "Put me in remembrance: let us plead together: declare thou, that thou mayest be justified."** Isaiah **48:3, "I have declared the former things from the beginning; and they went forth out of my mouth, and I shewed them; I did them suddenly, and they came to pass."**

God is in the same business today as He was then, He still brings things to pass, He is still God; He never changes, nor does He fail.

Are you looking for *some " suddenlys "* in your life? It is time that we, you and I, the whole body of Christ, start proclaiming, believing, desiring and, having faith in God. He can and He will demonstrate signs, wonders and miracles for us, if we just do our part!

Matthew 11:12, *"And from the days of John the Baptist until now the Kingdom of heaven suffereth violence and the violent take it by force."* In order for us to obtain our covenant rights, we have to take them by force. In order for us to "be a winner" over everything in life, over all of our mountains, all of our problems, we must learn to pray in the authority that God has given us in His Word. We have to take the Kingdom of heaven, by force!

The world is hungry, thirsty and searching for God by the millions. We have the answer to mighty miracles and profound demonstrations of God's power. We are "Heirs of God and joint heirs with Christ," which means that we share the same things with Christ. We have been given power over all the power of the enemy! That same *"winning power" that* Christ exhibited while He was on earth. **John 14:12,** *"...The works that I do shall he do also: and greater works than these shall he do."* When we were saved, God made available to us, all of His power, understanding, wisdom, might, and glory. Let us use the authority He has given us.

Ephesians 1:7, 8, "In whom we have redemption through His blood, the forgiveness of sins, according to the riches of His grace; Wherein He hath abounded toward us in all wisdom and prudence;"

Although we are thrust upon the battlefield of good and of evil when we are saved, God does not require that we go into battle alone. His Spirit dwells within us, so He directs and guides us. He leads us to victory! He has made us to be "winners!" He has authorized us to use His magnificent weapons, to defeat the enemy, every time! He has given us the whole armor of God and has instructed us to put it on in **Ephesians 6:10-13,** that we *"...may be strong in the Lord, and in the power of His might."* HE IS LETTING US USE HIS MIGHTY NAME, HIS BLOOD, HIS POWER, HIS SPIRIT, HIS AUTHORITY AND HIS WORD (which we know is God!). He also tells us in **Philippians 4:13** that, *"I can* *do all things through Christ which strengtheneth me,"* and in **Romans 8:37,**"...*in all these things we are more than conquerors through Him that loved us."*

When we live for God and obey His commandments, we will experience Victory over all things we call forth, by saying, speaking, and confessing the Word. **I John 4:4** tells us, the Greater One resides on the inside of us and that we are overcomers. *"Ye are of God, little children and have overcome them: because greater is He that is in you, than He that is in the world."*

All of our needs are met when we trust in, and believe on, the Lord. God is looking for more than just a few good men. He gave His life to bring salvation to all the lost. He demonstrated while on earth, the power that He left for us to use. He is looking for people who want to be winners, who will take dominion and become winners! This power that He left for us, is the greatest of all powers in the universe...with this power, we can do as Jesus did!

You ask, "How can we lose?" How can we lose if God is going to see to it that we win? The choice is ours. We lose, when we don't live for God and do His will by keeping His commandments. To understand the depth of one's loss that doesn't live for God, read **Deuteronomy 28:15- 68.** It is all written down very plainly for you; *"As for me and my house...we will serve the Lord!"*

In **Isaiah 42:6,** we are told, *"I, the Lord, have called thee in righteousness, and will hold thine hand, and will keep thee, and give thee for a covenant of the people, for a light of the Gentiles; To open the blind eyes, to bring out the prisoners from the prison, and them that sit in darkness out of the prison house."* And in the great commission, **Mark 16:15-17,** Jesus told His followers *"...Go ye into all the world, and preach the gospel to every creature. He that believeth and is baptized shall be saved; but he that believeth not shall be damned. And these signs shall follow them that believe; In my name shall they cast out devils; they shall speak with new tongues; They shall take up serpents; and if they drink any deadly thing, it shall not hurt them; they shall lay hands on the sick, and they shall recover."* And in **Acts 4:29,** *"And now Lord, behold their threatenings: and grant unto thy servants, that with all* *boldness they may speak thy Word, By stretching forth thine hand to heal; and that signs and wonders may be done by the name of thy Holy Child Jesus."*

God has given us everything we need to rise out of obscurity and defeat all the giants in our lives, just like David did. Let's become Giant Killers, just like David!

What belongs to us through our covenant and what is literally ours, is totally different. Every one of God's covenant promises are available to us and they belong to us as Christians. These covenant promises are ours when we stand, act on the Word and take them by force from the enemy. When we stand in our authority and take our dominion, God's promises are ours. God wants all of His covenant promises to be yours, and mine – He designed them for us. We are His children. They are part of our inheritance in Him. Our God wants us to be Winners! Praise God, He designed us to be winners!

In order to win, we have to fight the enemy. We have to take our promises by force! Let us advance God's Kingdom. Let us take all that He has for us. Let us take our healing, Let us take our loved ones out of the grip of the enemy. Let us take our wealth and riches and let us take all of our covenant promises! *Let us fight the good fight of faith.* In order to be able to take our covenant promises by force, we have to have a warring spirit concerning our enemies. We have to go to battle, and fight the devil and all evil forces for what is rightfully ours, by standing on God's Word.

I want to help you to be able to stand up and obtain all the good that God has available for you, as a Christian. Let me pray, and loose a spirit of war over you, to help you fight the good fight of faith.

A Prayer for Winners

I wear the whole armor of God that I may be able to stand against the wiles of the devil, with the Blood of Jesus covering me, from the top of my head, to the soles of my feet.

I now address, rebuke, and bind you, Satan, and every demonic spirit, including the prince of the air, away from each child of God who has read this book, and who desires to be a winner for the Lord, and I cast every one of you into outer darkness.

I bind and cast into the sea, every evil assignment against these for whom I pray, their causes and effects on all levels-spiritually, physically, emotionally, financially and socially. I break and reverse all curses against every reader who desires to be a winner for you, Lord. I declare that Satan is under their feet and is now dismissed, in Jesus' name.

I confess that their bodies are temples of the Holy Ghost and that they are redeemed, sanctified, cleansed, blood bought and justified, by the Blood of Jesus Christ. I thank you, Lord, for setting them free, in Jesus' name, Amen.

Dear Heavenly Father, I come before you to ask that a prayer mantle of a conquering, warrior spirit against all evil, be placed on every Christian who reads this book. Every person that has accepted you as their Lord and Saviour and confessed you before men, as we are instructed, in **Romans10: 9, 10.** *"That if thou shalt confess with thy mouth the Lord Jesus, and shalt believe in thine heart that God hath raised him from the dead, thou shalt be saved. For with the heart man believeth unto righteousness; and with the mouth confession is made unto salvation."*

I loose the anointing of God for victory to be placed on every saved reader to advance The Kingdom of God. That they might take it by force and fight for what is rightfully theirs. I loose the anointing of God over them, collectively and individually, to fight for signs and wonders, miracles of healings, restorations, wealth, riches, and all of their covenant rights.

It is time for all Christians to go forth, claiming their inheritances in the Lord. I loose the anointing of God for a prayer mantle and a warring spirit to be placed on all of these Christians, that they may go forth all over our country and over all the world; throughout every continent, island and tributary, as a *mighty army with a mission*; That they may take back, and be victorious over, whatever the enemy has stolen from them, their families, and their friends.

I loose upon them the anointing of God to fight the good fight of faith, and for the ability to call forth and stand on their covenant promises. I loose the anointing of God for a warring spirit, to give them the ability to pray victoriously, to speak God's Words with their mouths- words of protection, of abundant life, of total healing, wealth and riches.

I loose the anointing of God almighty upon them for the power, and the ability to be victorious in all things. I loose upon them the anointing of God to be a winner, all the days of their long lives. The guardian, bidding, ministering angels, and the angels of the Lord, are now loosed, to establish this earnest petition, these declarations and decrees; and to bring all this good to each of these, your Children, for your glory, Lord.

I bind all of their covenant promises, all of the wonderful blessings of God, to each of these who keep your commandments. I bind all of their heavenly promises and blessings unto them, and give thanks unto God, in the name of our Lord Jesus Christ. "… *be it unto them according to thy Word*," as in **Luke 1:38**. I thank you Father that each of these for whom I pray, are victorious and triumphant in all things, through Christ Jesus! It is established in Jesus' name. Amen, and Amen!

MIRACLE WORD MINISTRIES INT'L
ORDER FORM

Our Prayer is that
Pray Along Prayers
is a blessing in your life.

For re-orders write:
KEYSTONE PRODUCTIONS
P.O. Box 8838
Huntsville, Texas 77340

Please send Money Order for $19.95 + $6.95 for shipping
and handling for each book,
or order online @
Amazon .com
Or have your favorite bookstore order it for you.

Printed in the United States
67557LVS00006B/136-300